PATHFINDER
CAMPAIGN SETTING

Development Leads · Amanda Hamon Kunz and Jessica Price
Authors · Robert Brookes, Benjamin Bruck, Crystal Frasier, Thurston Hillman, Brandon Hodge, James Jacobs, Jessica Price, Patrick Renie, and David N. Ross
Cover Artist · Denman Rooke
Interior Artists · Leonardo Borazio, Sam Burley, Shen Fei, Miguel Regodón Harkness, Ralph Horsley, Warren Mahy, Jon Neimeister, Irina Nordsol, Will O'Brien, Jose Parodi, Kiki Moch Rizky, Firat Solhan, Florian Stitz, and Ben Wootten

Editor-in-Chief · F. Wesley Schneider
Creative Director · James Jacobs
Executive Editor · James L. Sutter
Senior Developer · Rob McCreary
Developers · John Compton, Adam Daigle, Mark Moreland, and Owen K.C. Stephens
Assistant Developers · Crystal Frasier, Amanda Hamon Kunz, and Linda Zayas-Palmer
Senior Editors · Judy Bauer and Christopher Carey
Editors · Jason Keeley, Lyz Liddell, and Josh Vogt
Lead Designer · Jason Bulmahn
Designers · Logan Bonner, Stephen Radney-MacFarland, and Mark Seifter

Managing Art Director · Sarah E. Robinson
Art Director · Sonja Morris
Senior Graphic Designer · Adam Vick
Graphic Designer · Emily Crowell

Publisher · Erik Mona
Paizo CEO · Lisa Stevens
Chief Operations Officer · Jeffrey Alvarez
Director of Sales · Pierce Watters
Sales Associate · Cosmo Eisele
Marketing Director · Jenny Bendel
Vice President of Finance · Christopher Self
Staff Accountant · Ashley Kaprielian
Data Entry Clerk · B. Scott Keim
Chief Technical Officer · Vic Wertz
Software Development Manager · Cort Odekirk
Senior Software Developer · Gary Teter
Project Manager · Jessica Price
Organized Play Coordinator · Tonya Woldridge
Adventure Card Game Designer · Tanis O'Connor

Community Team · Liz Courts and Chris Lambertz
Customer Service Team · Sharaya Copas, Katina Davis, Sara Marie Teter, and Diego Valdez
Warehouse Team · Will Chase, Mika Hawkins, Heather Payne, Jeff Strand, and Kevin Underwood
Website Team · Christopher Anthony, Lissa Guillet, Julie Iaccarino, Erik Keith, and Scott Spalding

On the Cover

Milani champions hope while Brigh contemplates invention and Zyphus heralds tragedy in this dynamic cover art by Denman Rooke.

Table of Contents

Reference

This book refers to several other Pathfinder Roleplaying Game products using the following abbreviations, yet these additional supplements are not required to make use of this book. Readers interested in references to Pathfinder RPG hardcovers can find the complete rules of these books available online for free at **paizo.com/prd**.

Advanced Class Guide	ACG	*Ultimate Combat*	UC
Advanced Player's Guide	APG	*Ultimate Magic*	UM
The Inner Sea World Guide	ISWG		

paizo

Paizo Inc.
7120 185th Ave NE, Ste 120
Redmond, WA 98052-0577

paizo.com

Introduction

From a simple farmer petitioning for a bountiful harvest to a young ruler seeking divine guidance to a brave adventurer relying on her goddess' power in the face of unfathomable evil, nothing permeates the world of Golarion more than faith. The divinities of the Pathfinder campaign setting are legion; in the lands surrounding the Inner Sea, the names and general portfolios of the core 20 deities are generally common knowledge, and their robust churches enjoy the greatest influence within those realms. This pantheon, however, is far from exhaustive in terms of the number of divinities whose worshipers call the Inner Sea region home.

This book details 15 of the lesser-known gods and goddesses who nonetheless offer great power to those who pledge their faith. The worship of these divinities in the Inner Sea region is less ubiquitous, but their histories, motivations, and schemes are no less wondrous than those of their more popular deific counterparts. This book provides all the tools to play a character—or create an NPC—dedicated to one of these mysterious divine beings, whether a deadly assassin pledged to Achaekek, the Mantis God; a brash privateer devoted to Besmara, the Pirate Queen; or a brilliant tinkerer committed to Brigh, the Whisper in the Bronze. The pages within also provide rules elements that allow devout characters to put their faiths into practice, including boons for characters with the Deific Obedience feat (see page 3) or levels in the evangelist, exalted, or sentinel prestige class (for details on each prestige class, see pages 198–203 of *Pathfinder Campaign Setting: Inner Sea Gods*).

The Gods' Power

Although the gods detailed in this book are sometimes colloquially referred to as minor gods, the term is something of a misnomer. They may be minor as far as their relatively smaller number of worshipers in the Inner Sea region, but they grant their followers just as much power and can affect the world just as potently as better-known gods. For example, a 9th-level cleric of Desna, a well-known major deity, is no more or less powerful than a 9th-level cleric of Naderi, the relatively esoteric goddess of drowning, romantic tragedy, and suicide, and both are able to cast 5th-level cleric spells.

That said, the Great Beyond's political landscape and the relationships among divinities are cosmologically complex and nuanced beyond the ken of mortal understanding. Some divine beings champion more fundamental or impactful concepts, dominate larger regions of the Great Beyond, or simply wield more influence or command more respect than their divine peers. Thus, divinities' relative power and standing within their respective pantheons varies wildly.

Like infinite, unthinkably mighty mortals, each divine being harbors various opinions and feelings toward her peers, and these outlooks influence the divinities' relationships, for better or worse. Divine beings have friends, allies, lovers, confidants, rivals, and enemies, but these bonds are often vastly more complex than mortal bonds. It is entirely possible, for example, for divine beings to be lovers and enemies simultaneously, or for them to have a tacit alliance that nonetheless leaves an overarching rivalry intact. In many cases, divine beings fall in and out of favor with each other, though the ripening or souring of relationships can take millennia. Temporary collaborations are usually much shorter, though they still might last one or two mortal lifetimes—merely the blink of an eye to immortal beings.

A divine being's age and deeds tend to influence her reputation among her peers. For instance, as one of the oldest creatures in existence and a potential cocreator of the multiverse, the draconic deity Apsu is afforded much respect in the Great Beyond, even if he is rather removed from and even uninterested in the happenings on the Material Plane. Similarly, Alseta, goddess of doors, transitions, and years, also enjoys immense regard thanks to her status as the gods' servitor and steward, as well as her work arbitrating their disputes. In contrast, some divine beings want little or nothing to do with their peers, and largely exist outside the politics of the Great Beyond. Achaekek the Mantis God, for example, maintains no long-term relations with other divinities, even though many of them have engaged his assassination services. Similarly, Groetus, God of the End Times, has little to do with other divinities, who find the maddening influence of his skull-moon concerning and carefully consider how they should approach him during the rare occasions they need to communicate with him.

Although it has no bearing on the power of spells and abilities granted to her followers, a divinity's status as a demigod or a full-fledged deity affects her standing in the Great Beyond. The number of domains and subdomains available to a divinity's clerics reveals his status; deities always grant access to five domains and six subdomains, while demigods grant four domains and four subdomains. In practice, this means that if clerics are devoted to a demigod as opposed to a deity, their options are slightly more limited, and their patron is more mysterious to the world's inhabitants. For all practical purposes, demigods should be considered a subset of deities.

Such a distinction is likely inconsequential to the details of a campaign, but knowing about a divine being's standing among his peers—and therefore how he may be motivated to guide his faithful—may inform the game's overarching story on a general level. Similarly, player characters may find themselves fascinated with divine lore, and Game Masters who reveal minute details about a divinity's standing or personal history in the Great Beyond can add a layer of mystery and depth to a campaign that would otherwise remain unexplored.

In some cases, the divinities detailed in this book grant access to subdomains without also granting access to the subdomains' associated domains. For example, Sivanah, the Seventh Veil, grants access to the Protean subdomain, but not to the Chaos domain. This exception to the rules, which normally allow a character to select a subdomain only if her god also grants its associated domain, is intentional, because it allows a god limited purview over a rather narrow element that is nonetheless vital to her nature. In the example above, Sivanah's alignment is neutral, and she therefore has no tie to the Chaos domain; however, her realm is in the Maelstrom, and she either hides from protean choruses or once was a protean herself, making her dominion of the Protean subdomain not only logical but suggestive to those who wish to uncover her many secrets. A character able to select a domain can take any subdomain granted by her divinity, even if the divinity does not also grant the subdomain's associated domain. The character receives all the abilities and spells normally granted by taking that subdomain, including the domain powers of the associated core domain that aren't replaced by the subdomain, even though the divinity cannot grant that core domain by itself.

Faith in Play

Just as this book's details about the gods' backgrounds, churches, priests, adventurers, and worship are intended to help Game Masters and players build worlds in which these divinities come to life, the rules presented in each section allow characters' faiths to become tangible factors in their lives and, in many cases, on the battlefield. Characters with the Deific Obedience feat, reprinted below, or levels in the evangelist, exalted, or sentinel prestige class can perform their divinities' obediences once per day to gain benefits and potential boons unique to their divine patrons. The divinities' obediences and boons are listed in their individual sections. Whenever an ability associated with a neutral divinity refers to a bonus, the type matches that of the character's bonus gained from performing her obedience—sacred or profane. For more information about the prestige classes, options or information related to divinities not covered in this book, and similar topics, see *Inner Sea Gods*.

Deific Obedience

Your reverence for a deity is so great that daily prayer and minor sacrifices grant you special boons.

Prerequisites: Knowledge (religion) 3 ranks, must worship a deity.

Benefit: Each deity requires a different daily obedience, but all obediences take no more than 1 hour per day to perform. Once you've performed the obedience, you gain the benefit of a special ability or resistance as indicated in the Obedience entry for the god to whom you performed the obedience.

If you have at least 12 Hit Dice, you also gain the first boon granted by your deity upon undertaking your obedience. If you have at least 16 Hit Dice, you also gain the second boon. If you have 20 Hit Dice or more, you also gain the third boon. Unless a specific duration or number of uses per day is listed, a boon's effects are constant.

If you have levels in the evangelist, exalted, or sentinel prestige classes (*Inner Sea Gods* 198–203), you gain access to these boons at lower levels as a benefit of your prestige class. If you have no levels in one of these prestige classes, you gain the boons marked as exalted boons. If you later take levels in sentinel or evangelist, you lose access to the exalted boons and gain access to the new boons appropriate to your class.

If you ever fail to perform a daily obedience, you lose all access to the benefits and boons granted by this feat until you next perform the obedience.

Achaekek

Achaekek, the Mantis God, exists to eradicate those who would usurp the gods' divinity. The god of assassins is a deadly hunter who strikes his targets unerringly, regardless of their strength or status. Some of the gods disapprove of Achaekek's amoral methods, but none have ever directly opposed the Mantis God. It is said that Achaekek alone can meddle in mortal affairs—but that may simply be a horror story other religions spread to keep their own faithful in check. In truth, no one knows whether Achaekek personally acts against mortals. Few, however, dare to test the old tales' veracity, for doing so might call down the Mantis God's bloody wrath.

HE WHO WALKS IN BLOOD

God of assassins, divine punishment, and the Red Mantis

Alignment LE

Domains Death, Evil, Law, Trickery, War

Subdomains Blood, Deception, Devil, Murder, Tactics, Thievery

Favored Weapon sawtooth sabre

Centers of Worship Ilizmagorti

Nationality monster

Obedience Meditate in a private place before a trophy or broken religious symbol taken from a target you have been contracted to kill. This trophy must be anointed with a single drop of your blood, drawn from your flesh by a sawtooth sabre, and the trophy must be destroyed at the end of your meditation. If you have yet to complete a contract, have no appropriate trophies at hand, or seek to serve the Mantis God in other ways than as the god's assassin, you must instead offer your own vital fluid to He Who Walks in Blood by cutting yourself along the right arm with a sawtooth sabre. Such self-mutilation deals 1d6 points of damage to you, which cannot be healed during the hour of meditation without disrupting the obedience; after the meditation ends, the wounds can be healed by any means available. You gain a +2 profane bonus to confirm critical hits while wielding a sawtooth sabre. As long as you have a sawtooth sabre in each hand, you can use those blades to complete the somatic component of any spell you cast, and you treat sawtooth sabres as your divine focus for the casting of divine spells.

> Achaekek's first victim was His creator. For the gift of saving us from this evil, all who live owe their lives to Him, and in time, He will come to collect from us all.
>
> —Anonymous

EVANGELIST BOONS

1: Blessing of the Mantis (Sp) *disguise self* 3/day, *invisibility* 2/day, or *gaseous form* 1/day

2: Walk Unseen (Su) He Who Walks in Blood cloaks your steps, ensuring that you can move clandestinely during your hunts. You are constantly under the effects of a *pass without trace* spell, unless you wish to be followed. You also gain a +2 profane bonus on Stealth checks.

3: Second Face (Su) Your deadly equipment is sacred to you. As long as you carry a *mask of the mantis* (*Pathfinder Campaign Setting: The Inner Sea World Guide* 298) on your person (even if you do so by carrying it in an extradimensional space), you can instantly don it as a free action or as part of an attack of opportunity. While you wear a *mask of the mantis*, you can attempt to demoralize a creature within 30 feet using Intimidate as a swift action. You no longer need to expend charges from a *mask of the mantis* to gain the effect of *deathwatch*, although you must expend charges as normal to use the mask's other effects.

EXALTED BOONS

1: Crimson Decree (Sp) *doom* 3/day, *death knell* 2/day, or *blood biography*^APG 1/day

2: Blood Scent (Sp) To your heightened olfactory senses, the acrid scent of blood is as pleasing and distinctive as the sweetest perfume. Three times per day, you can cast *blood scent* (*Pathfinder RPG Advanced Race Guide* 143) on yourself as a spell-like ability. This ability does not grant the spell's bonus on attack and damage rolls, even if you are an orc or have a rage ability.

3: Focused Assassin (Su) Your combat skills are just as deadly when you have an assassination target as when you don't. When you perform your obedience for the day, if you are not contracted to kill a target, you can name a single target. You need not know the exact name of your target, but you must know a suitably detailed and correct description, such as "the thieves' guild's second in command." Against that target, you gain a +2 profane bonus on attack rolls and weapon damage rolls, and you deal an additional 2d6 points of damage. The save DCs of any spells you cast on the target increase by 2. If you are contracted to kill a target, these bonuses apply against that target; if you are contracted to kill multiple targets, you must choose one target against whom these bonuses apply when you perform your obedience.

SENTINEL BOONS (ASSASSINS)

1: Blood Must Flow (Sp) *lead blades*^APG 3/day, *spiritual weapon* 2/day, or *keen edge* 1/day

2: Bleeding Wounds (Ex) All wounds you inflict with a sawtooth sabre are bleeding wounds, and deal 1d4 points of bleed damage to the target. If you deal bleed damage via another source (such as the bleeding attack rogue talent or by using a *wounding sawtooth sabre*), this ability does not deal additional bleed damage. You can also use *bleed* as a quickened spell-like ability three times per day.

3: Mantis Style Mastery (Ex) You take no penalties on attack rolls from two-weapon fighting when wielding two sawtooth sabres simultaneously, and you gain a +2 profane bonus on all damage rolls with sawtooth sabres. If you deal sneak attack damage with a sawtooth sabre, you deal 2 additional points of damage for each die rolled as part of your sneak attack damage. If you have levels in the Red Mantis assassin prestige class (*The Inner Sea World Guide* 282), the DC for the save against your prayer attack increases by 2.

UNDERSTANDING ACHAEKEK

Many theologians, including those who worship the Mantis God, agree that another god, or perhaps a group of them, created Achaekek—yet who exactly is responsible for his genesis is unclear. Certainly, the churches of Asmodeus, Calistria, Lamashtu, Pharasma, Rovagug, and Zon-Kuthon have compelling arguments that point to their patrons as the source of the Mantis God. Even the faiths of Norgorber and Gorum have legends that He Who Walks in Blood was born of their deities, despite legends of Achaekek originating far before either of them came to be. The most cogent belief may well be the one that the church of Achaekek espouses: that the creator of their god is long dead, murdered by the Mantis God for daring to create something so monstrous as himself.

Although known to his worshipers as He Who Walks in Blood, and commonly attributed by the faithful to be a masculine entity, Achaekek exists beyond conceits of gender, race, or politics. This means his followers come from enormously diverse backgrounds—united only in their common exaltation of the act of murder.

In art, Achaekek is universally depicted as a towering crimson mantis with four killing arms and a savage spike at the end of his long, slender abdomen. His eyes are endless pools of night, and he leaves a trail of blood wherever he walks, said to be from those countless victims the god and his cult have slaughtered over the eons. Achaekek is said to possess the power to rend reality itself in order to instantly travel to any time or plane to carry out missions of murder.

THE CHURCH

Achaekek does not actively seek worshipers, but as long as faith has existed, there have been those who see much to venerate and fear in the Mantis God's actions.

His only actively organized church on Golarion serves a dual role: the Red Mantis assassins are as much his holy servants as they are the most-feared guild of assassins in the Inner Sea region. Just as Achaekek does not directly strike against the gods, so do the Red Mantis assassins avoid contracts on the leaders of the mortal realm, seeing rightfully appointed monarchs as divinely appointed. All others are fair game.

The church of Achaekek, and thus the Red Mantis assassins' blades, are responsible for many famous slayings over the years. The deaths of those who aspired to divinity are perhaps the most well known, such as Arrogant Marsis, said to have been the most beautiful man in the world during the early years of the Age of Enthronement, or Yazanova, the murderous queen of the Tusk Mountains who sought to become the Goddess of the North. Yet the Red Mantis assassins were not always eager for such fame.

Achaekek's cult worked in secret for centuries in their homeland of Rahadoum. But in 2559 AR, on the eve of when the Laws of Man were to be enacted, the priestess Ximena received a vision from Achaekek. She led the Red Mantis to flee the Rahadoumi religious persecution, though the cultists were forced to give up most of their wealth in the flight. From that point on, necessity forced the Red Mantis to operate more openly, for the funds to remain hidden no longer existed. After centuries of piracy, the Red Mantis built up enough wealth to construct a city on Mediogalti Island; however, they did not wholly return to their secret ways. Today, their assassinations may be plotted in the shadows, but the results are left for all to see and fear.

Being home to the Red Mantis, Mediogalti Island is the center of Achaekek's organized worship. The cult is led by a group of deadly assassins known collectively as the Vernai, or "High Killers." Traditionally, there are 13 Vernai, mostly women; there are no restrictions against men in positions of power, but it is exceptionally unusual for a man to achieve the rank of Vernai.

The Vernai oversee all Red Mantis operations, approving every contract and organizing reprisals against traitors as needed, while simultaneously ruling the city of Ilizmagorti and managing its affairs. The Vernai themselves are ruled by one woman, the Blood Mistress, who is considered the ultimate authority on Achaekek's will. This role is for life, and has never been held by a man. The current leader is Blood Mistress Jakalyn, an ageless and passionate killer who supposedly has ruled the church and Mediogalti Island alike since the time of Aroden's death.

TEMPLES AND SHRINES

Most of Achaekek's worshipers are content to pray at secret shrines or improvised altars; these are often little more than alcoves marked with the god's symbol, or small structures housing trophies and broken emblems of faith taken from slain targets.

Not all of Achaekek's places of worship are so fleeting. In cruel societies, or nations where other lawful evil religions hold great power, smaller shrines exist openly, doubling as places the desperate or vengeful can go to contract assassinations. Achaekek's faithful have arranged special permissions to operate in such a manner in Geb and Nidal. In other nations, such as Katapesh or the River Kingdoms, shrines to the god of assassins are usually hidden in plain sight under the cover of other operations, even where no strict law against the church's operation exists. The cult is not well tolerated in Cheliax, for the Red Mantis's support of piracy along the western coast of Garund has long vexed House Thrune, but the church nonetheless maintains numerous secret temples throughout Cheliax.

The church's greatest temples are found on Mediogalti Island. In Ilizmagorti, the grand Pagoda of the Mantis stands proudly as one of the cult's cornerstones of worship, but the infamous Crimson Citadel, located deep in the isle's jungle interior, serves as the true house of power for the Red Mantis. The heart of the god's faith and the home of the Vernai, the Crimson Citadel is rumored to contain a mortal paradise, a collection of all the weapons and traps humanity has ever devised, the largest library in the Inner Sea region, and the deepest dungeons human hands have ever carved.

A PRIEST'S ROLE

While clerics of Achaekek certainly exist, many of the Mantis God's priests are not divine spellcasters. In order to progress above the rank of acolyte in the church, a non-divine spellcaster must prove her devotion by taking at least 1 level in the Red Mantis assassin prestige class (*Pathfinder Campaign Setting: The Inner Sea World Guide* 282). A priest of Achaekek who lives on Mediogalti Island is expected to perform some sort of public duty to protect or enhance the city, be it as a city guard, an architect, an artist who devotes her talents to the beautification of public works, or otherwise.

All priests of Achaekek are expected to serve as assassins should they have the opportunity to do so, regardless of their actual skills. As a result, most priests of Achaekek take either levels in the Red Mantis assassin prestige class or levels in another class that provides proficiency in such murderous pursuits (such as ranger, rogue, slayer, or the sentinel prestige class from *Pathfinder Campaign Setting: Inner Sea Gods*). Strangely, those who worship the Mantis God rarely take levels in the standard assassin prestige class—the church doesn't strictly forbid such a choice, but it is looked down upon

by most worshipers and usually marks someone who came to worship Achaekek later in life. Worshipers of Achaekek never ask for coin to defend or avenge themselves or their allies, but they believe fervently that assassins who kill for reasons divorced from personal interest deserve compensation for their services in recognition of their skills, and consider it an insult to be asked or told to kill someone without proper recompense.

Clerics of Achaekek can prepare *keen senses*[APG] and *negate aroma*[APG] as 1st-level spells and *spider climb* as a 2nd-level spell. Druids can prepare *murderous command*[UM] as a 1st-level spell.

ADVENTURERS

While the sawtooth sabre is not an uncommon weapon among adventuring and mercenary companies, the participation of an actual worshiper of Achaekek in such a group is rare. Most of those who join such groups generally do so for personal reasons, and they tend to keep those reasons—and often their

true faith—private. A worshiper of Achaekek, despite her adoration of murder and skill at killing, will never knowingly betray her adventuring companions. To do so is to invite the most terrible punishment in the afterlife, akin to that earned by slaying a rightful monarch.

Of special note are the rare heretics of Achaekek. These strange few worship Achaekek, but have openly disavowed the Red Mantis assassin guild, believing the assassins to have used the Mantis God to bolster their own mystique and reputation rather than advance the god's interests. The Vernai view these heretics as among the greatest of the church's enemies; however, the fact that Achaekek still grants magic to these unorthodox clerics implies there may be a kernel of truth to their beliefs.

These believers lead quiet lives and abandon the classic dress of the cult, yet continue to train with sawtooth sabres as they work to kill those who they believe deserve death. The heretics rarely accept payment for their deeds, believing that their actions keep fate on its proper course. These beliefs are not so different

from those who worship Norgorber as Father Skinsaw. However, openly commenting on this similarity draws swift punishment from heretical Red Mantis worshipers and Skinsaw cultists alike. Neither group admits any connection between their faiths, and in cases where they encounter one another, death is sure to follow.

CLOTHING

Achaekek's Red Mantis assassins employ distinctive armor and weapons. While their striking black-and-crimson leather armor of choice, when matched with their fearsome mantis masks, makes them unmistakable, it is the cult's signature weapon, the sawtooth sabre, that evokes the most fear. Even those who are unfamiliar with the ways of the Red Mantis find it difficult to mistake the curved, serrated blade of such a sabre for anything other than an instrument of swift death.

The assassins brutally hunt down any other than their own who wears the holy armor and mask of a Red Mantis assassin, but Achaekek's worshipers place no such bounties on those who train and master the use of the sawtooth sabre. This is perhaps because the wider these blades spread and the more they are associated with pain and death, the more notorious they become.

Rules for sawtooth sabres and the *mask of the mantis* can be found on pages 291 and 298 of *Pathfinder Campaign Setting: The Inner Sea World Guide*, respectively.

HOLY TEXT

Few modern religious texts make much mention of Achaekek, almost as if today's faiths have agreed to remain silent on the matter. Ancient texts, such as the mysterious *Book of Maan* and the *Path of Ways*, speak of Achaekek as a slayer of gods, yet the church currently holds that Achaekek slays no deities, and does not possess the ability to do so. Whether these ancient tomes speak of a time when the Mantis God may have served a different role is impossible to say, as no copies of them are known to have survived the intervening ages. If holy texts dedicated to Achaekek exist, they likely reside in the Crimson Citadel's mysterious Sarzari Library, to which only the Red Mantis's Blood Mistress has access. However, no copies of such books have ever been read outside of the cult, and the truth about their existence—and what secrets they contain—remain rumors to this day.

HOLIDAYS

Curiously, Achaekek's faithful hold no particular holidays or festivals as sacred. The induction of a new member into the Red Mantis is always a time for prayer, devotion, and revelry, and the successful completion of any contract is a time to give thanks to He Who Walks in Blood, but these events can take place anywhere at any time. Often, public holidays are selected as times to strike against those who have been marked for death, but this is done more for theatrics than because of any religious significance.

APHORISMS

Despite their focus on murder, Achaekek's worshipers follow ideals that, ironically, many would hold to be honorable and just.

Do Not Discriminate Against the Living, For in Death We Are All Equal: None shall be turned away from the faith on the basis of their gender, race, or politics, nor shall vengeance be sought for the same reasons, for death will visit all mortals and be the final arbiter. This belief may well be the one tenet of the faith that has stayed the Red Mantis's vengeful hands against Rahadoum, although the Red Mantis certainly do not ignore that land altogether.

Honor the Gods, For They Honored Us All with This World: The gods created this world, and they grant those who serve well in life boons in the Great Beyond. Speak not ill of the gods, and do not deny their power, for to do so is to mock and deny reality itself.

Let Death Be Final, For We Are Not the Keepers of Graves: One who dies should not be resurrected, particularly if her death occurs in the pursuit of the church's beliefs or as the result of a contract on the deceased's life. A worshiper of Achaekek rarely agrees to return to life if given the chance, and the god's worshipers generally do not perform spells such as *resurrection*, save in cases where not doing so causes a greater inconvenience or peril to the faith.

RELATIONS WITH OTHER RELIGIONS

Achaekek does not turn his claws against his divine sisters and brothers, and while many of the gods have engaged his assassination services, Achaekek keeps no relations with other deities. In Ilizmagorti, Besmara's faith is allowed, but largely as a concession to the city's dependency on piracy for support. Norgorber's faith is also allowed in the city, so long as those who venerate him as Father Skinsaw do not set foot on the isle—Achaekek does not tolerate this sect of the King of Thieves. The church respects the followers of Mephistopheles for his power over contracts, the value of which all assassins understand. Achaekek's faithful also respect Nocticula's followers, as they are the only assassins whose techniques the Red Mantis believe might rival their own in effectiveness. The Red Mantis lament, however, that these assassins are more of a cabal of talented lone wolves than an organized group.

Worshipers of Achaekek have prospered by avoiding aggression toward other religions—except toward Father Skinsaw's followers. While other good and lawful faiths might not approve of the methods the Red Mantis use, the church of Achaekek has always managed to remain less of a target of crusades than many other religions. Cynics whisper that even the gods of law and good, at times, have need of a slayer to handle the jobs that their own codes and morals won't allow, and that these deities instruct their churches to stay out of Red Mantis affairs on the off chance that the services of He Who Walks in Blood may be required in the future.

The only other significant relationship held by the cult of the Red Mantis is not with a religion, but with a philosophy. Achaekek's faithful still resent the exiling of their church from Rahadoum by the rise of the Laws of Man, and view that nation with a slow-burning anger. They have neither forgotten nor forgiven the ancient wrongs Rahadoum perpetrated upon them, and continue to watch and wait from Mediogalti Island. For now, the assassins seem content to take only actions involving observation and subtle meddling in trade and sea travel, yet whispers grow among those who worship the Mantis God that a reckoning may yet descend upon the so-called "Kingdom of Man." If these murmurs are to be believed, the entire nation of Rahadoum may one day be bathed in blood.

REALM

Achaekek is said to spend much of his time slumbering in the Outer Rifts, bathed in the blood of heretics and worshipers alike. This region is known only as the Blood Vale, a cavern filled with a crimson jungle and interlaced with a network of bloody rivers and swamps. It is said that the River of Souls brushes near to the Blood Vale, which opens from the Great Beyond at the base of the spire that forms Pharasma's Boneyard; from this vantage point, the Mantis God can watch as those slain in his name travel on to be judged. The Blood Vale is not part of Hell, Abaddon, or the Abyss, though rents in its razor-edged walls open into all three of these planes, providing shortcuts to those realms for those who visit the Vale. Achaekek also keeps dens on other planes, including in Hell's Avernus, and cracks in these dens are believed to allow the god to travel freely between them.

PLANAR ALLIES

As a deity granted special dispensation to work his will on the Material Plane, Achaekek does not keep many particular allies or favored minions, although his herald, Zyrruthys, is known to often speak for the god.

Zyrruthys (herald of Achaekek): Zyrruthys is a highly intelligent, enormous mantis, a crimson monstrosity often mistaken for Achaekek when he appears to wreak havoc on infidels. Zyrruthys particularly enjoys the destruction of villages or towns where large numbers of people have blasphemed or simply disrespected the Mantis God, and never asks for additional payment to perform such tasks, whether summoned by the faithful or dispatched by Achaekek.

Alseta

Alseta, the Welcomer, is the goddess of literal and metaphorical transitions. Doors, hidden passageways, and the flow of time all fall under her purview. She fills a unique role among Golarion's gods, not only serving as the gods' steward, but also acting as an intermediary both among the respective gods and between the gods and their followers. Alseta's dominion over doorways and thresholds also makes her the goddess of teleportation and planar travel. In this aspect, many elves revere her as the patroness of the *aiudara*, or elf gates. This kindly guardian goddess treats all beings with respect and, in turn, enjoys reverence from members of nearly all faiths.

THE WELCOMER

Goddess of doors, transitions, and years

Alignment LN

Domains Community, Law, Magic, Protection

Subdomains Arcane, Defense, Home, Inevitable

Favored Weapon dagger

Centers of Worship Absalom, Brevoy, Lastwall, Taldor

Nationality Taldan

Obedience Find a physical boundary between two places, such as a doorway, a bridge, or even just a line drawn in the sand. Kneel with your back to this boundary and contemplate all the ways your life has changed during the previous day—this could be as simple as a new person you met in passing. Stand, turn, and step across the boundary while chanting a prayer to Alseta. On the other side, kneel and meditate on the transitions and changes that await you in the coming day. At the end of this meditation, out of respect for the transition to the new day, vow to perform a mundane task in a distinctly different manner during the coming day than you have done previously. You then gain a +4 sacred or profane bonus on Disable Device checks to unlock doors and a +4 sacred or profane bonus on Perception checks to detect secret doors. The type of bonus depends on your alignment—if you're neither good nor evil, you must choose either sacred or profane the first time you perform your obedience, and this choice can't be changed.

> Praise Alseta the opener! May she open the path to virtue and wisdom. Praise Alseta the closer! May she close the path of iniquity and strife.
>
> —The Sacred Keystones

EVANGELIST BOONS

1: **Keeper of Keys (Sp)** *hold portal* 3/day, *knock* 2/day, or *glyph of warding* 1/day

2: **Safe Passage (Ex)** Alseta smiles upon your attempts to clear away obstacles that would hinder travelers' passage. You do not risk triggering a trap while attempting Disable Device checks unless you fail your check by 10 or more, rather than by 5 or more as normal. If the trap is part of a door or archway, or is otherwise triggered by passing through a door or archway, you gain a +4 sacred or profane bonus (of the same type as that provided by your obedience) on your Disable Device check.

3: **Summon Door (Sp)** You have an uncanny knack for acting as a holy gatekeeper against those who would stand against you. Three times per day, you can use *passwall* as a spell-like ability. When using this ability, you also conjure a strong wooden door (hardness 10, hp 40, break DC 30) at one end of the passageway produced by the spell. The door has a lock requiring either a plain iron key (which magically appears in your possession) or a successful DC 30 Disable Device check to open. You can also conjure the door so it comes into being already unlocked and open.

EXALTED BOONS

1: **Warden (Sp)** *alarm* 3/day, *arcane lock* 2/day, or *greater stunning barrier*ᴬᶜᴳ 1/day

2: **Turning of the Seasons (Sp)** You have a deep understanding of your goddess's connection to teleportation. Once per day, you can use *teleport* as a spell-like ability. When you use this ability, increase your familiarity of your intended destination by one step (a place you've viewed once becomes a place you've seen casually, a place you've seen casually becomes a place you've studied carefully, etc.). Using this ability cannot result in a mishap; if you roll a mishap on the spell's table when determining how well the teleportation works, treat it as a result of a "similar area."

3: **Eviction (Sp)** The Welcomer trusts your judgment enough to grant you powerful magic to keep your enemies at bay. Once per day as a standard action, you can bar all creatures from passing through a specific door or entrance within 30 feet of your position. This functions as the spell *antilife shell*, except that it functions on all creatures regardless of their type. This effect lasts a number of rounds equal to your Hit Dice. If a creature trying to penetrate the barrier has spell resistance, you must overcome that resistance in order to keep it out. You can use your Hit Dice in place of your caster level on this spell resistance check.

SENTINEL BOONS

1: **Watchful (Sp)** *line in the sand*ᴬᶜᴳ 3/day, *mirror image* 2/day, or *countless eyes*ᵁᴹ 1/day

2: **Past and Future (Ex)** You catch glimpses of the future that allow you to avoid your enemies' strikes. You gain improved uncanny dodge as a rogue of a level equal to your Hit Dice. If you already possess the improved uncanny dodge ability, or if you would gain it later, you instead gain a +2 sacred or profane bonus (of the same type as that provided by your obedience) on attack and damage rolls against creatures that are currently flanking you.

3: **Portal to Safety (Sp)** Once per day as a standard action, you can transform an open door or archway into a temporary one-way portal, connecting it to another open door or archway of your choice that you have seen or of which you have a reliable description. This portal functions as a *greater teleport* spell targeting any creature that passes through the first doorway until the end of your next turn. All creatures that pass through the doorway, up to the limit imposed by the spell and your Hit Dice, arrive at the same location, and the destination must include an open door or archway from which the targets exit.

PALADINS OF ALSETA

As the intermediary between and servitor to the other civilized gods, Alseta prefers to remain neutral in conflicts among the gods. This impartiality naturally extends to her faithful, and thus followers of Alseta rarely become paladins.

The elves of Kyonin are a noteworthy exception to this trend. Elves who revere Alseta as the patron goddess of the *aiudara* (or "elf gates") swear oaths in her name to defend these sacred elven relics from those who would visit destruction upon them, including the fiendish Treerazer and his demonic forces. In addition to the normal paladin code, the tenets of these elven paladins of Alseta include the following affirmations.

- Doorways are sacred boundaries and should be respected. I will not transgress across the threshold of an occupied structure uninvited unless doing so serves the glory of Alseta or is necessary to prevent a great evil from taking place.
- The *Sovyrian Stone* is a blessing from the goddess and is the beating heart of the elven people. I will defend it with my life.
- The aiudara are sacred relics and should never be used lightly. It is my responsibility to preserve the knowledge of the keys to these gates, and ensure they do not fall into the wrong hands.

UNDERSTANDING ALSETA

Alseta acts as a guardian of boundaries. She strengthens city gates, shields guards from invaders' arrows, and turns away unwelcome visitors. Alseta is also a guardian of metaphorical boundaries, particularly those related to time and life. Those celebrating birthdays or marriages or embarking on new ventures often invoke Alseta's name. Expectant mothers and mourners of the dead alike often pray to Alseta in the same breath as Pharasma, and indeed, some consider the Welcomer and the Lady of Graves' faiths intrinsically linked.

Alseta appears as a kindly human woman dressed in simple gray clothing, and she wears a smiling mask on the back of her head. She is even-tempered and considers her words carefully; when she speaks, she does so with an authority and poise that soaks into the very bones of listeners. Alseta is, above all, courteous and treats all beings, from the humblest peasant to the mightiest of the gods, with respect and civility. In return, she expects the same from any who deal with her, and has little patience for those who do not practice such courtesies.

Those who earn Alseta's favor find that physical blockades often open easily to them, or that metaphorical obstacles melt away more easily than expected. They uncover new opportunities in unexpected places, and receive flashes of insight that illuminate options that otherwise wouldn't have occurred to them. Those who displease the goddess find themselves barred at every turn or feeling as if they were stuck in ruts. Doors jam when being opened, and swing loose to admit drafts when they should hold fast.

Alseta's holy symbol is a woman's face in profile, facing left, wearing a smiling mask on the back of her head.

THE CHURCH

The church of Alseta is best known for the abjuration services it provides. For a fee, Alsetan priests will enchant locks to resist picking, ward a building against teleportation, and set magical traps to deter or slay unwelcome guests. While these spellcasting services provide the church with most of its income, they make up but a small part of the church's regular activities.

As Alseta serves the gods, so does her church serve its community. Temples of Alseta open their doors to visiting dignitaries and provide neutral meeting grounds for enemies to resolve disputes. Alsetan priests officiate weddings and other civic ceremonies, mediate negotiations, and witness the signing of important documents. The church of Alseta also inspects and maintains city walls and gates, ensuring they remain strong enough to repel both humanoid enemies and rampaging monsters. Alsetan temples and priests work closely with local constabularies, offering discounted healing and spellcasting services to any individual harmed in the course of defending the city's gates. At the neighborhood level, Alsetan priests bless the thresholds of houses and other personal residences to keep them safe from hostile forces.

Most followers of Alseta are courteous and civic-minded; they are often hosts, negotiators, diplomats, seneschals, or otherwise involved in formal and informal administration. The most popular professions among her faithful tend to be barrister, diplomat, magistrate, and city guard. People join the church looking for ways to support and strengthen their community, and members must commit to community service as part of their initiation into the faith. This usually takes the form of acting as a concierge for the temple or as a door greeter before services. For petitioners more talented in manual endeavors, repairing public doorways is a popular project.

The church of Alseta is not as rigid or hierarchical as that of most lawful gods. This is in part because her local flock is rarely large enough to sustain such a hierarchy; additionally, her worship is mostly informal, with prayers whispered during times of transition and over the dedication of doorways rather than in formal services. Where temples exist, the top-ranking priest is called the high chamberlain; this priest directs the church's activities and organizes lower-ranking priests into whatever order she deems necessary. Priests operating outside of a temple's influence are called chamberlains, and are technically subordinate to the nearest high chamberlain. In practice, though, they tend to operate at their own discretion.

Services to Alseta are usually processional in nature. At larger houses of worship, these begin with a group prayer on the church's front steps, after which the gathered worshipers proceed, single-file, into the temple. As worshipers pass through the temple's chambers, they reaffirm their faith in the goddess. The devotees linger in the main sanctuary and listen to a sermon before exiting on the temple's opposite side. They end the service with a second group prayer.

TEMPLES AND SHRINES

Few temples are dedicated solely to Alseta, but small shrines to the Welcomer are ubiquitous in many places. They can adorn city gates and bridges, entryways and arches, and the major streets' cobblestones, invoking the goddess to guard these edifices from invasion or disaster. Many also keep small shrines to Alseta in their homes, hoping the goddess will safeguard them from intruders and thieves. Freestanding shrines to Alseta are less common. These serve a functional purpose as well as a religious one and take the form of sundials or stone calendars.

Where they do exist, temples of Alseta are elaborate buildings designed in honor of the goddess, celebrating her through architecture with numerous rooms, trapdoors, and hidden passages. The temples have an almost labyrinthine aspect; rooms in the temple always have multiple exits, and hallways connect back to themselves to form endless loops. Each temple includes a main hallway that follows the building's perimeter. Priests carry icons of the goddess and symbols of the changing months and seasons around this hallway in grand processions to celebrate the equinoxes, solstices, and the turning of months and years.

A PRIEST'S ROLE

Priests of Alseta are generally outgoing paragons of courtesy and fair-mindedness. This makes them excellent hosts, negotiators, and diplomats, and many are also members of local governing bodies. Alsetan priests are famous for their equitable dealings with members of other faiths, and many call upon the Welcomer's priests for aid or succor when members of their own church can't be found or trusted. Churches of other faiths sometimes hire priests of Alseta to bless the entrances of their temples, resolve interfaith squabbles, and bear witness to important ceremonies. The Welcomer's clergy members have a particularly sterling reputation among the clergies of Pharasma and Abadar—given a choice, many of these would rather employ Alseta as an arbiter than Asmodeus, who always has his own wicked interests in mind.

Alseta's priesthood is primarily made up of clerics, though a surprising number of fighters also venerate the Welcomer. The latter are usually former members of the city watch who are no longer fit to fight, but who still wish to serve their community. Good-aligned and neutral rogues interested in locks and traps also make up a large portion of Alseta's priesthood.

Good-aligned priests see themselves as guardians of their community. They serve without expectation of reward, although donations are always welcome. Evil-aligned priests tend to be cunning trap-masters who enjoy watching their cruel implements mangle and torture would-be intruders. They are equally committed to their community, but may express this devotion as xenophobia or paranoia directed at neighboring communities. Neutral clerics tend to apply themselves to civic improvement or governance for the sake of pure order.

Beyond the abjuration spells an Alsetan priest performs for hire, the blessing of thresholds is an important part of his duties. This usually involves placing a small statue of

the goddess above the doorway, or otherwise inscribing images of Alseta and prayers to the goddess on the doorway's lintel. Many priests of Alseta thus have some skill in stonework or sculpture, and a good number have ranks in either Knowledge (engineering) or Craft (sculptures). Anyone can petition the church to bless the doorway of a home or business, and priests typically perform these services for free or at the cost for any statuary used.

A typical day for an Alseta priest begins with prayers, which coincide with the rising sun. Most clerics prepare their spells at this time. The day is further divided with prayers at noon and at dusk. The timing of these prayers is of prime importance to the faith, and all priests must set aside other activities to perform these rituals. By the faith's tenets, even adventuring priests must perform these prayers unless doing so places them in mortal danger. Particularly devout priests may mark the passing of each hour with its own small ritual.

Clerics of Alseta can prepare *open/close* as an orison, and can prepare *arcane lock* and *knock* as 2nd-level spells.

ADVENTURERS

Most of those drawn to worship the Welcomer are interested in peaceful pursuits, such as law, architecture, or diplomacy. However, some faithful possess the courage and drive to pursue the adventuring life. Curiosity prompts these brave souls to explore dungeons locked behind long-sealed doors, or to cross the unfathomable thresholds between the planes. Others seek to seal doors that never should have been opened, closing rifts to the chaotic planes or ensuring that terrible monsters do not escape to threaten the civilized realms. Some take this philosophy a step further and view undeath as a metaphorical door that should never be open to creatures, and these followers of Alseta make it their mission to destroy undead, thus closing that door many times over.

While Alseta blesses many of her followers with the ability to open locked doors with ease, she also expects her faithful to exercise this power with restraint. This makes her faith a poor fit for those interested in breaking and entering or committing other illegal acts. Alseta's church is often popular with members of the city watch, and many of the adventurers who worship her also come from the ranks of the constabulary.

CLOTHING

Priests of Alseta garb themselves in brown and gray clothing, preferring simple or old-fashioned styles to more modern or flamboyant designs. The highest-ranking or wealthiest members of the clergy may wear vestments tastefully embroidered with shimmering copper or silver thread. Arch and key motifs are common, and priests favor subtly symmetrical patterns.

The masks Alsetan priests wear on the backs of their heads are their most identifiable feature. Each mask is unique, carved by its owner at the time of her initiation into the church, and represents some aspect of the priest's past gladly left behind by joining the priesthood.

HOLY TEXT

Alseta's holy text, *The Sacred Keystones*, is an allegorical document comparing personal virtues to the four traditional keystones used to support the arches of an Alsetan temple's main entrances. The four major virtues emphasized in the text are courtesy, duty, honesty, and humility. Many other traditional virtues are derived from these four primary ones, and are represented by different stones in the arch. Although it is mainly a text on morality, *The Sacred Keystones* employs several extended architectural metaphors, and many passages provide genuine insights into the fields of architecture and engineering.

HOLIDAYS

The church of Alseta helps organize many of the other civilized gods' festivals, but adherents also celebrate one of their own. In addition, transitions between months are minor holy days.

Turning Day: This festival celebrates the end of the old year and the beginning of the new, taking place at midnight on 31 Kuthona. On Turning Day, celebrants forgive old debts and grudges and embrace new opportunities. Friends reaffirm their bonds, and longtime enemies exchange gifts in hopes of reconciliation. Turning Days marking the end of centuries or millennia are especially extravagant affairs, and may last much longer than their name implies.

APHORISMS

The following aphorisms are drawn from Alseta's holy book, *The Sacred Keystones*.

A Door Must Open: Short for "A door must open; otherwise, it is not a door," this expression reminds Alseta's faithful that a skill or tool left unused has no value. Some adventurous members of Alseta's faith take this saying literally, and endeavor to carefully open the long-sealed doors of dungeons or ruins to give them purpose.

Turning the Mask to It: Figuratively, this expression means leaving something—an attitude, feeling, grudge, or material possession—in the past, but carrying the memory, or mask, forward with you.

RELATIONS WITH OTHER RELIGIONS

Rather than pursuing her own goals, Alseta primarily acts as a servitor to the other gods. When the gods meet, Alseta often serves as the gathering's host. When they argue, she serves as the arbiter of their disputes. When the gods need someone to act as a steward to their realms, they trust in Alseta to secure their holdings in their absence. For this reason, Alseta remains on polite, though not necessarily friendly, terms with most of the civilized gods.

This attitude extends to the members of Alseta's faith, who get along cordially with the followers of most other gods. In fact, the priests of other gods sometimes include prayers to Alseta at the beginning of important ceremonies to open the way between the mortal realm and the realm of the gods. Priests of Alseta do their best to maintain the same neutrality as their patron goddess.

Alseta has a particularly close relationship with Pharasma. This is likely due to the overlap between the two goddesses' portfolios, as death is but the soul's transition between the mortal world and the afterlife. The strong alliance between Alseta and Pharasma has led some scholars to suggest that Alseta was once a mortal servant or worshiper of Pharasma. Others suggest that Alseta was a powerful psychopomp who rose to godhood in much the same way that Sarenrae rose from the ranks of the angels to true divinity. These scholars point to the mask that Alseta wears on the back of her head, noting the similarity to the masks that psychopomps wear.

One might expect some tension between Alseta and Pharasma's enemies, particularly Urgathoa and Zyphus, but this is rarely the case. Alseta's track record of impartiality has earned her the trust of even these deities. Beyond that, Abadar likes and respects Alseta, as they are like-minded on many issues. Of the major gods, only Rovagug and Lamashtu regularly act with hostility against Alseta. These monstrous deities represent the violent, barbarous hordes battering at the doors of civilization; the servants of Alseta oppose the activities of these deities, and are not averse to combat when words fail to dissuade them.

REALM

Known as the Argent Gate, Alseta's realm is an ornate gate and adjoining temple located on a massive piece of solid silver floating through the Astral Plane. Some speculate that it was once a part of the Eternal City of Axis, but that Alseta moved it to avoid making gods of other alignments uncomfortable. Regardless, the Argent Gate is a powerful artifact capable of creating portals to almost anywhere in the Great Beyond. Combined with its location on the neutral ground of the Astral Plane, this makes the Argent Gate an ideal location for meetings of the gods.

PLANAR ALLIES

Alseta commands respect among the planes, and all but the most chaotic or wicked outsiders are willing to aid her followers, provided that they are properly compensated. The following are some of Alseta's best-known servants and can be summoned using spells such as *planar ally*.

Inzorth (unique blink dog): This two-headed blink dog hunts those who abuse teleportation magic to bypass justly erected barriers. Legends say that it can track teleporting creatures by scent, and that its bark disrupts dimensional travel. Inzorth grows irritable with those who do not treat both its heads with equal deference, and any gift offered to Inzorth must be divided or doubled so that each head receives an equal portion. When addressed singularly, its left head is called "Inz" and its right is called "Orth."

Lockmaster Pylaethus (unique axiomite): Pylaethus is one of the finest locksmiths among the planes. Rumor has it that he once studied as an apprentice under Abadar himself, but parted ways with the Master of the First Vault for reasons unknown. He now serves Alseta, securing the Welcomer's gates and doors with locks of unparalleled craftsmanship and complexity, particularly in the rare event when the goddess needs a door to remain closed. Pylaethus's most treasured possession is his collection of strange and unusual keys, and he is often willing to perform favors for mortals in exchange for new specimens to add to his collection.

The Welcoming Faces (herald of Alseta): This enormous, construct-like outsider appears to be masks of copper and silver tied together, as if around an invisible head. Each face wears a small, enigmatic smile, even while the creature speaks, which is often. The Welcoming Faces frequently appears to powerful followers seeking guidance on whether to open a particular secured door or whether to embark on a life-changing transition—for the wisdom of passing such thresholds is often of deep concern to Alseta, and thus to the Welcoming Faces. On rare occasions, the Welcoming Faces also appear to defend temples of Alseta from particularly powerful or evil intruders. The Welcoming Faces also serve as an arbiter between powerful mortals who disagree over a fundamental issue, such as the boundaries of nations or conflicting laws governing access to pilgrimage or heritage sites.

Apsu

Apsu, the Waybringer, is one of the oldest and mightiest creatures in existence. According to Apsu's faithful, he and his mate, Tiamat, spawned the dragon-gods who created the whole world. He remains a father figure to almost all dragons, whom he loves as his children, and to those who count dragons among their progenitors, literally or figuratively. The exception is the faithful of his murderous and destructive son, Dahak, with whom Apsu anticipates a final and terrible reckoning. For this reason, the good-aligned dragons and all those who fight for the interests of his loyal draconic progeny continually pray to the great Apsu, trusting in his inevitable righteous victory.

THE WAYBRINGER

God of good dragons, leadership, and peace

Alignment LG

Domains Artifice, Good, Law, Scalykind, Travel

Subdomains Archon, Construct, Dragon, Exploration, Toil, Trade

Favored Weapon bite or quarterstaff

Centers of Worship Absalom, Taldor, Triaxus

Nationality dragon

Obedience Pick a direction, and walk that way for the next 30 minutes. During this time, catalog all of the areas you pass and consider any tactical advantages that can be found in the terrain. After this, retrace your steps, but instead of plotting tactics, appreciate the beauty and scenery that you find along your way, and speak quiet prayers to or praises of the Waybringer, keeping in mind that none of what you've seen would exist were it not for Apsu. You then gain a +2 sacred bonus on Perception checks while you are traveling in this area, and a +4 sacred bonus on checks to notice enemies for the purpose of acting in a surprise round while you are traveling or camping there.

> I shall protect, for
> I am Apsu. I shall fly
> the skies, waiting
> for my son. Our
> battle draws close;
> the time is nigh.
> I shall be victorious,
> for I am Apsu.
>
> —Draconic Apsu

EVANGELIST BOONS

1: Maker's Ways (Sp) *floating disk* 3/day, *align weapon* (law only) 2/day, or *tiny hut* 1/day

2: Touch of the Artificer (Su) You have discovered divinely inspired lines of primordial energy—gifts from Apsu, you believe—that can imbue weapons with bursts of magic. Up to three times per day, as a standard action, you can touch a single weapon and grant it the *dancing* property for the next 3 rounds. A single weapon cannot be targeted by this effect more than once per day.

3: Crafter's Pride (Sp) You have learned the intrinsic nature of what gives life to objects, and can pour your soul into the construction of a given creation to infuse it with a semblance of blessed life. Once per week, you can cast *animate objects* on a single object that you've created. The effect does not have a duration; the animated object remains indefinitely as a companion, following your commands as best it can. You cannot animate a new companion while one is already serving you, though as a full-round action you can dismiss a companion, reducing it to lifelessness. If your companion is destroyed, you cannot use this ability again for another week. You cannot affect an object animated in this way with a *permanency* spell.

EXALTED BOONS

1: Waybringer's Ingenuity (Sp) *blurred movement*[ACG] 3/day, *levitate* 2/day, or *haste* 1/day

2: Eyes of the Pursued (Su) You adhere to Apsu's dictate of living to fight another day, and you've mastered the art of monitoring places you've left. Anytime you use a teleportation effect to move, you can place an invisible magic sensor in the area from which you just departed. As long as you are on the same plane as the sensor, you can see and hear everything occurring within 30 feet of the sensor as a swift action. The sensor lasts for a number of rounds equal to your Hit Dice. You can have a maximum number of active sensors equal to your number of Hit Dice.

3: Homeward Bound (Su) As a follower of Apsu, you deeply understand the importance of having a safe place to which you can retreat; you've come to count on several safe homes, creating ties to them when necessary. Once per month, you can designate a location to be your refuge. Once per week as a full-round action that provokes attacks of opportunity, you can teleport yourself and any willing creatures within 30 feet of you to the safe home of your choice, regardless of distance, as long as it is on the same plane. You can have a maximum number of refuges equal to half your Hit Dice. As long as none of your allies are in a refuge, you can remove its designation as a safe home as a swift action, but if you do so, you can never again designate it as a safe home.

SENTINEL BOONS

1: Exiled's Wrath (Sp) *color spray* 3/day, *scorching ray* 2/day, or *draconic reservoir*[APG] 1/day

2: Apsu's Shroud (Su) Apsu smiles upon your martial prowess and protects you with a halo of divine energy from his distant realm. You gain a +1 sacred bonus to your Armor Class, which increases to +2 against attacks from evil-aligned creatures. This bonus increases to +3 if the attacker is an evil-aligned true dragon. If an evil-aligned true dragon confirms a critical hit against you, the creature must succeed at a Fortitude save (DC = 10 + 1/2 your Hit Dice + your Charisma modifier) or be blinded for 1 round.

3: Chromatic Scourge (Su) You channel the righteous and immortal fury of Apsu into your weapon, making it ready for the endless fight against Dahak and his wicked allies. Once per day as a swift action, you can imbue your weapon with the hidden wrath of Apsu. If your target is evil, you gain a +20 profane bonus on your next single attack. If your opponent is an evil-aligned creature of the dragon type, treat your next single attack roll as both an automatic hit and a critical threat. You gain a +4 profane bonus to confirm the critical hit.

APSU'S PALADIN CODE

Paladins of Apsu valiantly follow the dragon god's tenets of holy vigilance against evil. Those following the rigid code of a paladin must sacrifice the sedentary lifestyle of living in a single place in exchange for continuous travel and hardship. The tenets of such paladins include the following maxims.

- I am the talon of Apsu's wrath. I strike where I am needed, but only when evil has been unmasked and there can be no doubt of my enemy's malice.
- When my purpose is unclear, I will walk the roads of the world to find a fresh focus. Every road leads to a new beginning.
- Nothing is worth sacrificing my life for, except protecting the lives of others. I will retreat when needed, and come back to vex my foes once again.
- Mercy is offered, but only once. Should I be betrayed in my moment of kindness, I will not stop until I have put my enemy down.
- It is not enough to slay evil and carry on. I will spend the time necessary to help those I've protected to fend for themselves.

UNDERSTANDING APSU

According to draconic lore, in the beginning of time there flowed two waters, fresh and salt, which became Apsu and his mate, Tiamat. The couple spawned the dragon-gods who created all the mortal world, but their first child, the destructive Dahak, traveled to Hell to revel and rampage, turning it into a place of darkness and ever-burning fire. Dahak then struck out at his siblings, destroying each in turn; the shattered remains of these draconic gods formed the first metallic dragons, who were cast onto the Material Plane as mortals. This enraged the fresh water, who realized that he must take a name so he could descend upon the Material Plane to confront his son. The fresh water then declared the immortal words: "I shall then be Apsu, for I am the first."

Aiding Apsu in his quest against Dahak were the god's metallic dragon children. The ensuing battle eventually saw Dahak laid low, but at a terrible price, for many of the dragons had sustained dire injuries. Just as Apsu prepared to strike the killing blow against his son, Dahak called out to his mother, the great salt sea. Unwilling to see her first son perish, the still-nameless sea offered to heal the battle's brutalized survivors in exchange for their efforts to save Dahak's life. Weakened and suffering, some accepted, exchanging goodness for evil, and battle raged between the metallic and chromatic dragons.

Dahak escaped his father's claws, and though the metallic dragons were poised to pursue, Apsu bade them to save their rage for another day. He then asked his mate why she aided their treacherous son, but she merely named herself Tiamat, mother of all—a name that still brings pain to all dragons—and held Apsu responsible for the deaths of her children. Tiamat then expelled him from their primordial realm, and Apsu vowed that, one day, he would make his stand against Dahak.

Apsu and Dahak's bitter enmity has since been the source of discord among the dragons of the cosmos. Apsu has accepted the inevitability of a final conflict with his son, choosing, for unknown reasons, the world of Golarion on which to make his last stand. Apsu's avatar is a dragon dwarfing the largest of the great wyrms, a regal and magnificent sight to behold. His silver scales sparkle with a pearlescent glow. When in this form, Apsu guides dragons and mortals alike, preparing all for the day his final battle with Dahak will commence.

THE CHURCH

Apsu's connection with Golarion is mostly focused on the knowledge that this world will host the final battle against his son. Dahak, either out of fear or a rare moment of foresight, has chosen not to force the conflict. Instead, agents of both deities act in small ways on Golarion, attempting to prepare for the inevitable conflict to come. Apsu's draconic-focused background results in a lack of any centralized church for his worshipers on Golarion— the closest such organization is a group called the Platinum Band.

The Platinum Band is a tight-knit group of Apsu devotees with two official offices: one in the Taldan city of Oppara, and the other a consulate in the Puddles district of Absalom. Members are recruited into the organization from among those who know and respect the history of Apsu and Dahak. The group is primarily made up of humans, with a handful of other humanoid races, as members of those races who learn of the impending battle between the dragon gods most likely favor Apsu's side and the defense of all life in the cosmos. The Platinum Band offers structure to the actions of Apsu's mortal worshipers, even if it's not a formal church, with senior members maintaining the organization's meager holdings.

Periodically, bronze dragons who have spoken directly with Apsu visit the band's representatives in human form to pass along important messages from the god, who rarely, if ever, speaks to non-dragons. Some say this is because humanoids could not handle the power of Apsu's unadulterated voice without descending into madness. Others say the god simply believes that humanoids, particularly humans, are too fickle or insufficiently invested in Apsu's faith to warrant his direct communication with them.

Among the dragons of the Inner Sea region, many pay homage to Apsu. However, typically only bronze and gold dragons maintain any direct connection with their deity, with bronze dragons serving as emissaries on behalf of Apsu while gold dragons act as the paragons of Apsu's beliefs. The latter also hold the power to call convocations of dragons, which all but the most sullen black dragons attend. Sometimes gregarious brass dragons serve as Apsu's servants and diplomats, though they don't tend to be particularly religious. Apsu's faith isn't limited to the metallic dragons, though—even some of the most vile chromatic dragons venerate and pledge support to Apsu, who can appear to his followers as any type of dragon and with any features he wishes.

Several organizations dedicated to Apsu's cause lie beyond Golarion, the nearest being on Triaxus. On that world, members of the Dragon Legion are trained to work with dragonkin (*Pathfinder RPG Bestiary 5* 98) in defense of their territories. Those inducted into the ranks of the Dragon Legion are often trained in the teachings of Apsu, though their leaders prohibit priests from revealing their patron's connection to Golarion, fearing that such knowledge may tempt younger soldiers to prematurely attempt the journey to that world to assist their deity's efforts. Instead, the Dragon Legion on Triaxus hopes to one day raise a grand army to offer to Apsu on the eve of the dragon's final conflict with the merciless Dahak.

TEMPLES AND SHRINES

The architecture of sites devoted to Apsu is largely dependent on location. Such sites are rare on Golarion, where formal religion is relegated to lone dragons or small bands of humanoids. Most temples or shrines to Apsu are stone affairs with gold and platinum holy implements and sturdy stone daises and altars. A vast polished mirror embedded in the ground rests at the center of each shrine, overseen by a large silver statue representing Apsu. Otherwise, the Waybringer has little in the way of codified standards for his sites of worship. Worshipers reflect on their achievements while looking into the mirror, ensuring that the battle against evil has not driven them from the path of good.

Apsu's primary and best-known temples are floating silver, gold, and platinum monoliths contained within his personal demiplane realm. The only

features on these solid, imposing structures are a few peninsular landing pads, each sized to allow a Colossal dragon to land on or take off from it. The interiors of these free-floating sanctuaries are lit with a vibrant, silvery light.

A PRIEST'S ROLE

Priests of Apsu follow myriad paths, but his few humanoid followers most often take levels in cleric, paladin, or warpriest. Apsu has no oracles, for he believes inflicting a curse on a living creature is a terrible crime against that being, even in exchange for divine power. Dragon servants of Apsu have little need for class levels, as most of their kind simply progress through their natural age categories. Draconic followers of Apsu tend to believe that a dragon's natural progression is far superior to superficial training, anyway.

Priests of Apsu don't have a standard daily routine, instead traveling the world in search of threats against dragonkind, or directly resulting from the actions of Dahak's worshipers, against whom they wage a constant struggle in preparation for Apsu's coming battle. Apsu's priests can be found almost anywhere, following up on leads relating to Dahak's actions and those of his minions. Luckily, the rarity of Dahak's agents on Golarion gives priests plenty of leeway in pursuing their deity's greater agenda.

Apsu's relative obscurity means his priests oftentimes must explain their religion to others who they encounter on their missions, as most places on Golarion aren't familiar with the Waybringer. In doing so, they may forge connections with the settlements they visit, which they reinforce by offering Apsu's divine gifts to those in need, or even settling in a goodly community for a time to help protect its residents.

ADVENTURERS

The majority of Apsu's Golarion-based, non-draconic priesthood are adventurers. Some discovered a tome or scene of draconic carnage that revealed the dire nature of the struggle between Apsu and Dahak. Others were inspired by the dying words of a devotee of Apsu to take up the mantle of battle against the forces of Dahak. Followers of Apsu typically specialize in confronting evil dragons, but they fight evil

wherever it can be found. They follow no specific creed, other than believing in the punishment of the unjust and continuing the constant battle between good and evil. They hold that in the end, Apsu will lead all goodly folk to victory.

One of the less-prominent directives of Apsu's teachings is the establishment of fortifications against evil. Counter to the dungeon-delving many associate with adventurers, some worshipers of Apsu travel the world to build and strengthen defenses. These architects find settlements, especially those with nearby draconic threats, and help reinforce those communities against aggressors. They leave their mark across the breadth of the world, rather than a single location, often combining their calling to build impressive fortifications with Apsu's affinity for travel.

CLOTHING

Followers of Apsu cover themselves in metallic armor or clothing with a metallic sheen. Many of Apsu's supporters mistakenly associate their master with platinum, but silver is actually Apsu's most favored

color. Both bronze and gold are used as accents on armor; the former is used in poorer communities while gold is seen on only his wealthier followers and priests. Humanoid priests typically wear a gold or silver brooch in the shape of a dragon's foot; alternatively, they might carry other custom-made equipment of that shape or bearing that image.

HOLY TEXT

The *Draconic Apsu* is the definitive holy text of Apsu, despite having been written by the now atheist and blind gold dragon sage Gunnarrex. The dragon wrote the text of the 4,000-line epic in one continuous sitting, in part as an apology for accidentally stumbling into Apsu's realm, the Immortal Ambulatory, at an inopportune time. Apsu strongly supports the meaning behind the text, which includes verses on the nature of good and evil and the creation of dragonkind. The *Draconic Apsu* foretells the coming of the final battle between Apsu and Dahak, but does not detail it.

HOLIDAYS

The following holidays are sacred to Apsu's faithful.

Time of Reminiscence: Apsu's followers spend the first day of winter in solitude, remembering past events, allies, and lovers. This holiday is symbolic, representing the time Apsu spends thinking of the ways the world has changed since his first offspring were born.

Wanderer's Escape: The first day of summer is meant to be a day of travel. Servants of Apsu spend this day and the following week in the wilderness, traveling across unknown lands. By doing so, the practitioner becomes acquainted with new hiding spots and defensible positions.

APHORISMS

The following sayings are common among the Waybringer's church and his faithful.

It Shall Be Made: Architects serving the designs of Apsu often espouse this verse. It is commonly employed when receiving a request to build an important structure, but followers also say it when making a promise to create something physical or metaphorical.

To Returning: Used frequently as a salute for those servants of Apsu venturing off into the unknown, this verse is used in everything from barrooms to temples. Uttering the phrase is often accompanied by the raising of one's weapon or the wave of a hand, and a small smile.

RELATIONS WITH OTHER RELIGIONS

Apsu's contact with other deities is sparse, the result of draconic strife being so far removed from the worries of other gods, but he maintains stronger relationships with good-aligned deities, particularly those of a lawful bent. Iomedae and Torag are supporters of Apsu, as is Sarenrae, who remembers the contribution of dragonkind in the act of shackling of Rovagug within his prison. Other deities pledge minor support to Apsu, particularly Cayden Cailean and Gorum; the former opposes evil and thinks the coming battle between Apsu and Dahak "will be a good rumble," while the latter eagerly views the coming draconic war as a vast conflict in which his forces can fight (on either side).

The dragon god Dahak is Apsu's first progeny and greatest enemy. Ever since Dahak engineered the destruction of the original draconic pantheon, Apsu has fought his wayward son. Both dragon deities know their final battle approaches, and Dahak is constantly preparing for this world-shaking confrontation. Despite their impending conflict, they had civil discourse in the aftermath of Rovagug's imprisonment, when Dahak told his father why he had decided not to betray the other deities and Apsu made his proclamation of eternal protection over Golarion.

Asmodeus is the only evil-aligned god known to approach Apsu, and has offered his services for some unknown price and reason. Apsu remains civil with the Lord of Hell, but has thus far rebuffed him each time. Dahak's spies within the Immortal Ambulatory report that Asmodeus has offered to weaken Dahak before the start of the dragons' final battle, though other claims state that the Archfiend has also made a similar offer to the Endless Destruction.

Following her completion of the Test of the *Starstone*, Iomedae approached Apsu. Having researched the noble dragon deity, she sought to involve Apsu more deeply in mortal affairs and ally with him in the struggle against the evil deities of the cosmos. Apsu's dogged determination to one day battle his son in the skies of Golarion prevented any long-term alliance, but Iomedae still left the attempt with a friend in Apsu. The two gods agreed to defend one another should they ever come under attack by other deific powers. Iomedae's divine servant Peace through Vigilance, a unique celestial gold dragon, is considered the physical manifestation of the agreement between the two gods.

REALM

The spherical, floating demiplane known as the Immortal Ambulatory is Apsu's realm. Vast islands glide within the sphere, each the ultimate destination for the souls of a different type of metallic dragon. A multi-environmental island floats at the edge of the realm, home to the few chromatic dragons who serve Apsu in his home domain. The Opalescent Cathedral rests on an island at the center of the Immortal Ambulatory. Apsu resides in this massive, shining structure, piloting his realm across the Great Beyond with his draconic allies at his side. The Immortal Ambulatory freely wanders the breadth of the Great Beyond, but is most often found within the boundaries of the good-aligned planes, especially Heaven.

PLANAR ALLIES

Many of Apsu's allies predate the existence of some of Golarion's other gods. The following are his best-known servants, and can be summoned using *planar ally*.

Blameless Flame (unique couatl): One of Apsu's oldest allies, Blameless Flame is wreathed in the righteous fire of a gold dragon's breath weapon. He travels the Material Plane in search of texts or items that spread the creed of Dahak, immolating such items in holy fire. In doing so, he weakens Dahak's church significantly, for with the eradication of each text, fewer are able to learn of the Endless Destruction.

Oregenus (herald of Apsu): This graceful, celestial adult silver dragon is easily recognizable because of the enormous spectacles he always wears. Oregenus is as kind as any of his species, but he is also somewhat aloof from the needs of the people he protects as Apsu's herald. He serves Apsu by traveling to the Material Plane to construct fortresses and shelters for those living near malign dragons or powerful evil threats, delivering heartening words from the god along the way. Oregenus's breath weapon is unique in that it leaves behind a permanent block of ice, akin to a *wall of ice*, which the dragon can sculpt into longstanding structures. However, the silver dragon's ice does not radiate cold and has the same hardness as stone, making it incredibly useful as a protective shelter for those the herald wishes to house.

Syrax the Platinum (unique clockwork dragon): Neither chromatic nor truly metallic, Syrax is Apsu's emissary, traveling the breadth of the Material Plane and Great Beyond in service to her master. The leader of the old empire of Thassilon, Emperor Xin, had an abiding interest in clockworks up until his death. This clockwork dragon (*Pathfinder RPG Bestiary 4* 30) is the result of one of the emperor's forgotten experiments, an attempt to take the mind of a brass dragon and transplant it into a mechanical body. Syrax managed to escape from Xin's control just after the procedure and made her way to the Immortal Ambulatory, where she begged for Apsu to reverse the process. While the draconic god could not aid her, he did remark on her incredible spirit and charged her with traveling the Material Plane and the Great Beyond as his emissary.

Besmara

Besmara, the Pirate Queen, is the proud patron goddess of corsairs and sea monsters. While brash, lusty, confrontational, and greedy, she follows a code of honor and is loyal to her crew and allies—so long as doing so serves her interests. She cares little for senseless murder or other unprofitable acts, but is willing to risk much to attain great prizes. She has little influence or interest in the mortal world beyond the sea and its immediate reach. Besmara doesn't care about clashes between good and evil, only pursuit, battle, and reward. Thus, even the most irreverent pirate captain throws a share of treasure overboard now and then as tribute to the Pirate Queen.

THE PIRATE QUEEN

Goddess of piracy, sea monsters, and strife

Alignment CN

Domains Chaos, Trickery, War, Water, Weather

Favored Weapon rapier

Centers of Worship Garund, Ilizmagorti, The Shackles

Nationality Kellid

Obedience Steal a gold coin or alcoholic drink by force or trickery. Then, while recounting your latest or most impressive act of piracy and blessing Besmara's name for all to hear, offer your stolen item to her by throwing it into water at least 4 feet deep. Alternatively, you can recount your most impressive or recent act of piracy to someone unaware of it, although you are free to hide the fact that the act was yours. You then gain a +2 sacred or profane bonus to AC against attacks of opportunity. The type of bonus depends on your alignment—if you're neither good nor evil, you must choose either sacred or profane the first time you perform your obedience, and this choice can't be changed.

> Carve your name on the ever-changing sea with a blade of terror and triumph. Fight for plunder, fame, and glory, and earn your place among the legends of the sea.
>
> —Besmara's Code

EVANGELIST BOONS

1: Tricky Adversary (Sp) *illusion of calm*ᵁᶜ 3/day, *daze monster* 2/day, or *twilight knife*ᴬᴾᴳ 1/day

2: Coerce Service (Su) You understand and can exhibit the blatantly charismatic pull of your goddess, convincing others to aid you even if they normally might not. Once per day, when you attempt a Diplomacy check to bribe a target (treat as if you are attempting to improve an NPC's attitude toward you by one step) or an Intimidate check to coerce a target, you can use this ability to gain Besmara's blessing to ensure further cooperation. You gain a +4 sacred or profane bonus (of the same type as that provided by your obedience) on the Diplomacy or Intimidate check, and if you succeed, the target is immediately subject to a *geas/quest* effect. For as long as the effect lasts, you can concentrate as a standard action and learn whether the target is actively undertaking your orders or actively defying them.

3: Bribed Sea Monster (Sp) The sea monsters at Besmara's behest follow your call at the goddess's command. Once per day as a standard action, you can summon one of the monsters Besmara has bribed or intimidated into aiding her followers. You must choose the monster from among the following list: adult sea dragon (*Pathfinder RPG Bestiary 3* 96), sea serpent (*Pathfinder RPG Bestiary* 244), or vouivre (*Pathfinder RPG Bestiary 4* 270). The monster appears as if summoned via *summon monster*, and you must summon it into an appropriately watery environment. It follows your commands perfectly for 1 round per Hit Die you possess before vanishing. The monster doesn't follow commands that contravene Besmara's interests, such as blocking waterways or giving a navy better control of a sea region; issuing such untenable instructions, if they're egregious, could cause the monster to attack you.

EXALTED BOONS

1: Captain's Bluster (Sp) *command* 3/day, *aggressive thundercloud*ᴬᶜᴳ 2/day, or *wind wall* 1/day

2: Treacherous Mirage (Sp) Besmara's blessing allows you to hide the truth once per day. This ability takes the form of either *false vision* or *mirage arcana*. You can change the illusion by spending a move action in concentration. The illusion lasts until you create a new one or dismiss this effect as a swift action.

3: Rally Crew (Su) The Pirate Queen lends you her divine panache, which fills all of your allies with courage and pride in their service to you. Once per day as a standard action, you can inspire all allies within 60 feet to greater speed and might. They each gain a 10-foot bonus to their speed and the benefits of *heroism*. On any attack rolls, saving throws, or skill checks benefiting from this morale bonus, your allies take no penalties due to the effects of water or weather. The bonus lasts for 1 hour per Hit Die you possess. As an immediate action, you can cause any number of creatures who disobey your orders to lose this bonus.

SENTINEL BOONS

1: Fearsome Boast (Sp) *monkey fish*ᴬᶜᴳ 3/day, *slipstream*ᴬᴾᴳ 2/day, or *water breathing* 1/day

2: Doom of Sailors (Sp) You can immobilize ships or scatter a fleet with a wave of your hand. Once per day, you can cast either *control water* or *control winds*.

3: Pirate Queen's Curse (Su) You know that the Pirate Queen's enemies are destined to suffer, and you can deliver her wrath personally. Three times per day, you can channel a curse through your weapon. You must declare your use of this ability before you make the attack roll. On a hit, the target is cursed unless it succeeds at a Will saving throw to negate the effect (DC = 10 + 1/2 your Hit Dice + your Charisma modifier). The curse causes the target to be sickened for a number of days equal to your Hit Dice; furthermore, during this period, any creatures flanking the target or against which it is denied its Dexterity bonus to AC deal an additional 1d6 points of damage with every successful hit. This extra damage applies to the attack that delivers the curse. In addition, all creatures with a swim speed have a starting attitude of hostile toward the target. This is a 7th-level curse effect. The curse cannot be dispelled, but it can be removed through *break enchantment*, *limited wish*, *miracle*, *remove curse*, or *wish*.

BESMARA'S ANTIPALADIN CODE

Antipaladins of Besmara are cutthroat pirates, freely roaming where they will and seizing whatever interests them. They primarily emulate their goddess's violent aspects, but different antipaladins focus on varied aspects of Besmara's code. The code of Besmara's antipaladins includes the following adages.

- I pursue what I desire. One who cannot keep it from me does not deserve to possess it.
- Treasure demonstrates my might. I won't waste my time on schemes with no profit to be had.
- No trick is beneath me. I will never forgo an advantage in the name of fairness.
- Pride does not shackle me. I retreat if I must to survive for another day.
- The weak serve the strong. I will never let my crew forget or doubt my strength.
- Revenge can be delayed to keep the ship sailing. Crew members who cross me shall die onshore; foes can be useful allies under changed circumstances.
- I will suffer no restraint. Those who seek to pacify me will fall broken in my wake.

UNDERSTANDING BESMARA

Originally, Besmara was a powerful water spirit with an affinity for manipulating sea monsters. She gained fame among primitive tribes who bribed her to drive these creatures toward rival coastal villages; later, when tribes began boat raids on other settlements, she could be bribed to send her monsters to fend off these attacks or arrange for predation-free sailing for the aggressors. Sometime before the Age of Enthronement, after long playing both sides, she consumed rival spirits of wood, gold, and battle to become a minor goddess. Her influence has since waxed and waned alongside the naval powers of coastal empires. Besmara is content with her current level of strength and notoriety and knows she cannot unseat a more popular deity (though if she had such an opportunity, she just might take it), so she entertains herself by raiding the outposts of celestials, fiends, and minor divinities.

With a buccaneer's heart and mind, Besmara follows a simple personal code. She gives chase if she wants something, but if she decides she can't win, she retreats. She allows her prey a head start if she wants a challenge, but hardly believes fights have to be fair. She thinks nothing of betraying someone who is no longer useful to her or teaming up with an old enemy for a common purpose. However, she despises anyone who tries to restrain her, her activities, or piracy in general.

The Pirate Queen appears as a brash, raven-haired pirate captain of any race she pleases, flamboyantly dressed—typically in colored pantaloons, black boots, a blousy shirt, and a hat (a bicorne, tricorne, or bandana). Despite her inhuman origins, she does not take any monstrous forms, even when angered, though swarms of sea creatures have been known to crawl out of her clothing to do her bidding.

Besmara's favor takes the form of gold coins spinning, mists concealing one's approach from enemies, enemies dropping weapons or having their weapons misfire, and opposing ships' sails tearing or burning. She shows her anger through stored food spoiling in a matter of moments, potable water turning to sludge, peg-legs and hooks irritating their wearers, foul-smelling winds, and an increased presence of sea monsters.

THE CHURCH

Besmara's followers are greedy folk. While some take to the seas in search of adventure or for the joy of exploration, most such folk gravitate to more benign gods, so Besmara's flock consists mainly of those who lust for treasure above all else. Such followers covet the belongings of others—whether actual riches, property, titles, fame, or lovers—and think it's fair for them to take what they want. Most are chaotic and love their personal freedoms. Her followers hate staying in place day after day, and are usually content to spend only a few days carousing in town before setting sail again. Like Besmara, her followers enjoy strife more than peace—when two nations are squabbling, Besmarans can plunder both and blame the attacks on the victims' rivals.

The Pirate Queen's followers have many superstitions about good luck (cats, figureheads with open eyes, pouring alcohol on a deck), bad luck (whistling on deck), and evil spirits (wearing gold jewelry wards them off) in addition to other traditions and beliefs. They say those who oppose Besmara feel seasick on the water and hungover on land.

There are no formalized rituals common to all churches, but services are generally upbeat, with singing, boot-stomping, dancing, and the lighting of incense or matches (particularly slow-burning matches and fuses). Burials are one of the few somber occasions, marked by a short prayer and either burial at sea (with the body weighted down with a chain, cannonball, or heavy-but-inexpensive treasure) or burning a rowboat or raft bearing the corpse.

Besmara has few priests, for pirates are more superstitious than religious, but she counts among her followers anyone who has made a desperate prayer to her when facing death on the sea or given tribute to gain her favor. Nearly all of Besmara's followers are pirates or pirates by another name. The rest are, along with a few intelligent sea monsters, folks who profit from strife—such as war profiteers, dog fighters, and similar low-class individuals—officials in "pirate towns," pirates' spouses, and prostitutes whose clientele comprises mainly pirates.

While such folk may rarely or never set foot on pirate ships, they indirectly profit from successful piracy, and pray to Besmara that their favorite buccaneers return with plenty of coins to spend. Some Besmaran hookers and rent boys consider themselves "sacred prostitutes" of the goddess, though this devotion often consists of little more than a "pirate queen" costume and roleplayed seduction (antics at which the goddess laughs). Male prostitutes among the faithful are often referred to as matelots (a term also sometimes given to the male spouse of a pirate).

As is befitting a chaotic pirate goddess, the church has no official stance on marriage, offspring, or raising children. Some pirates never marry, some have many spouses, and some have children, which they may choose to acknowledge or train. Very few in the faith embrace celibacy, save those with an obvious disfiguring condition or venereal affliction.

TEMPLES AND SHRINES

Given Besmara's small priesthood, there are few with the time and interest to build temples to her. Most of her temples are repurposed buildings or shipwrecked hulls, some of which are half-submerged. A public temple always displays a jolly roger flag, and its priest fences goods and sells healing potions, local nautical charts, and hideout tips. In places where piracy is frowned upon, these temples have a public purpose (such as selling rope or barrels), and knowledge of their true nature is shared among pirates by word of mouth.

Far more common than temples are shrines to the goddess. In port towns, these shrines may be merely nooks between buildings with a pirate flag and a carving of Besmara or an old ship's figurehead. These shrines usually have a cup or a place to hold a stick of incense or a match. When a petitioner pours rum or grog into a shrine's cup, it trickles out of a hole in the bottom or through a channel in the figurine's arm so it appears the goddess is drinking the offered beverage. A priest living on a ship usually owns a portable shrine that doubles as an altar, and may store it in her quarters or display it on the deck where suddenly pious pirates can mutter a prayer mid-battle.

A PRIEST'S ROLE

There is essentially no hierarchy within Besmara's church—each priest crafts his or her own title and recognizes no authority other than the goddess. Priests don't report to anyone, though they may defer to a mentor if they lack a good reason not to do so. Rarely does a particular ship have more than one priest on board, and in those cases they are often rivals. Every few years, a charismatic priest-captain may unite other like-minded priests under his or her banner, creating an armada with the leading priest as the admiral, but this is rare.

Most priests are practical folk rather than zealots, using their magic to gain advantages on the water. This is not to say that a typical priest's belief isn't sincere, but there is a marked difference between the crazed devotion of a Lamashtan cleric or the noble serenity of an Iomedaean paladin and the utilitarian faith of a Besmaran priest. As long as the goddess is respected and gets her fair share of tribute, she is content with little more than lip service, and her priests know this. By using her magic to gain wealth, power, and fame, they serve her interests and demonstrate her greatness.

Like lay worshipers, Besmara's priests are either pirates or folk whose business directly relies on piracy. Their personalities run the gamut from dashing privateers to rapacious murderers, and some in the middle may play both roles as the mood or pay suits them. They bless pirates and ships, heal crews, act as go-betweens for those looking for work or workers, guard pirate ships, chase off or bind sea monsters, and ever strive to profit from their activities. Most priests consider it undignified to abandon fallen allies to be eaten by a sea monster—after all, crewmates depend on each other, and a sailor cannot pay the priest for healing if he perishes— unless doing so would save other crew members from an early death.

Priests of Besmara are usually skilled at Heal and Profession (sailor). Most have ranks in Acrobatics, Appraise, and Intimidate. Canny followers also have ranks in Diplomacy, Knowledge (geography), Knowledge (history), Knowledge (local), and Knowledge (nature). Priests don't have any set routine, though most follow the normal cycle of activity on ship. Daily prayers are short and to the point.

Besmara's holy symbol in most seas is a skull and crossbones on a black or red field, though Ulfen pirates often instead

use a Viking helm with crossed swords behind it. Nearly all of Besmara's priests are clerics or rangers, with a few bards and druids, though every few decades an antipaladin champions her more destructive aspects. Clerics of Besmara can prepare *lesser geas* as a 4th-level spell and *curse of disgust*UM as a 5th-level spell, but can use them only to cause aversion to boats, ships, or open bodies of water.

ADVENTURERS

Devout adventurers serve Besmara by keeping the high seas unpredictable enough for the Pirate Queen to attract plenty of worshipers and see many exciting adventures. They often seek out lone naval vessels or other official ships to plunder; such victories can quickly build a devout adventurer's reputation as a brave buccaneer. The devout

also take pains to learn whatever they can about their patron deity's sea monsters—just in case.

Most adventuring followers of Besmara are pirates in some sense or another, and indeed work in an even wider variety of roles than her priests do. Most know how to seize a ripe opportunity for quick profit or glory and the value of being able to get away when a retreat is wise. Besmara blesses both righteous privateers battling the Chelish navy and murderous buccaneers who give no quarter to defeated opponents—much like the war god Gorum, her interest is in the conflict, not the consequences of its resolution. Her followers have been known to stir up trouble by sailing aggressively (or even attacking) while using a temperamental nation's colors or falsely claiming to be "legitimate privateers" as they attack in peacetime.

CLOTHING

Besmara's priests wear clothing that is functional on the high seas, yet that is also distinctive enough to help opponents recognize them and hence build their reputations as buccaneers. As a result, their wardrobes vary widely. However, most try to incorporate some sort of visually distinctive element, such as billowing black-and-white pantaloons or ruffled blouses.

HOLY TEXT

On water, text is difficult to keep safe, so Besmara's clergy do not keep much in the way of holy texts.

Besmara's Code: The Pirate Queen's holy text is just a few pages detailing treatment of crew, treasure, and captives. Most priests who can read make copies in their own hand; those who cannot read memorize the text's key points and ignore what doesn't concern them.

HOLIDAYS

The church of the Pirate Queen possesses no official holidays, though the ones listed below are commonly celebrated among Besmara's followers.

Harmattan Revel: This simple celebration marks the ebbing of sahuagin attacks at the start of winter.

Reefclaw Moon: The second full moon of summer in northern Garund marks the annual return of dangerous migrating reefclaws, preventing raids by all but the luckiest or most powerful buccaneers.

APHORISMS

These three phrases are the core of the goddess's code.

End Your Quarrels on Shore: Whatever disagreements one sailor has with another, onboard a ship is not the place to settle them, for everyone's survival depends on the crew working together.

Thirty Stripes Lacking One: The traditional punishment for a serious infraction on the ship is thirty lashes on the bare back. The captain or boatswain, however, may choose to reserve the last (30th) lash as an act of mercy if the target is repentant or unconscious. If so, the captain retains the option to make that last strike at any time before the ship reaches port—a threat to ensure better behavior from the target.

Truce Ends at the Horizon: Breaking a truce is seen as not only unsportsmanlike, but a threat to all pirates—but any truce is valid only until the opposing ship is past the horizon. This gives the weaker captain a head start should he fear the other captain's intentions.

RELATIONS WITH OTHER RELIGIONS

Besmara is a thorn in the side of many lawful powers and a casual ally or enemy of just about everyone else. Like her followers, she interacts peacefully when it suits her, but may betray an ally when it is convenient or profitable. She has been known to associate with Cayden Cailean, who considers her dangerously attractive; Gorum, who respects her strength and devotion to battle's excitement over its causes; Gozreh, who calls her sister, partner, and monster-tamer; and Hanspur, with whom she sometimes sails on raids (see page 63).

Erastil dislikes Besmara because she eschews tradition, and because she values brashness over benevolence. Iomedae finds the Pirate Queen's corrupt sense of honor distasteful. Abadar abhors her because she disrupts naval trade, and Asmodeus despises her because she has no sense of order, dares to interfere with his plans, and disrespects him. Because her home is in the Maelstrom, she frequently interacts with protean cabals, but has bargained and bribed them into accepting her presence.

In her relationship with sea monsters, Besmara plays the clever bully who keeps other bullies in line through physical threats and force of personality. Her monsters are like vicious dogs who reluctantly obey her command to heel only because she can hurt or kill them. Aquatic races usually venerate their own gods and avoid attracting her attention, for her monsters prey under the sea as well as upon it. Besmara's worshipers are accordingly encouraged to use her reputation to help them intimidate aquatic foes, but must take care not to overreach themselves. While she may bless a boasting follower if she likes his attitude, that follower must to some extent be able to stand against such creatures on his own for her blessing to do him any good.

REALM

Rather than a defined realm, Besmara wanders the chaos of the Maelstrom aboard her idealized pirate ship, the *Seawraith*. While depictions of it vary with the observer's cultural notion of a warship—everything from a galleon to a longship to a junk—the *Seawraith* inspires fear and respect. Besmara can change its appearance and configuration at will, as well as the environment around and within it. This power extends only about a hundred yards from the ship itself. Fortunately, the ship's mobility and her chaotic powers make it very difficult to find should she wish to be hidden, and several vengeful divine entities have sought her in the Maelstrom for centuries, only to give up in frustration. Sometimes Besmara leads an armada of petitioner-crewed ships or drags floating wreckage, loot, and crazed, undying sailors in her ship's wake. The *Seawraith* is also a constellation in Golarion's sky.

PLANAR ALLIES

Most of Besmara's best-known minions are great beasts from beneath the waves. Besmaran priests all know of legendary, dead pirate captains and may call them with the right bribe, but most prefer to conjure nightmare creatures to drag enemy sailors to their deaths. The following are well-known supernatural servitors of Besmara and can be summoned using spells such as *planar ally*.

Blackwarn (unique decapus): This tentacled, stealthy creature resembles a bear-sized aquatic decapus (*Pathfinder RPG Bestiary 2* 77) encrusted with barnacles. Its preferred payments are gold, squid brains, or gnome flesh.

Kelpie's Wrath (herald of Besmara): This storm-battered pirate vessel has the skull and spine of a great sea creature mounted on the prow, and eerie lights flicker on its deck and stream from its masts. The ship is the source of many horror tales of abandoned ships found in the ocean or spectral ships crewed by ghosts, but it is actually a living creature. On the rare occasions when it comes to the mortal seas at Besmara's bidding, it appears to punish some buccaneer for a horrid blasphemy against the Pirate Queen. Left to its own devices, it sails mortal waters, the Ethereal or Astral Planes, or strange dream-realms in search of plunder, danger, and glory. When called by mortals, it demands treasure as payment for its services, preferring chests full of gems and gold. It has a lecherous, voyeuristic streak and might lower a price for anyone willing to give it a carnal show. If properly bribed, it serves with grudging loyalty until the task is done, then leaves.

Old Vengeance (charybdis): This ancient charybdis (*Pathfinder RPG Bestiary 2* 56) has been under Besmara's thumb since before she was a goddess. Old and weary, it persists out of spite and the hopes that someday it will see the Pirate Queen destroyed. It loves the taste of creatures drowned in holy or unholy water.

Rusizi (unique dragon turtle): Alternately described as a turtle, a crocodile, or a dragon turtle with a crocodilian head, this huge creature is sometimes worshiped as a god by lizardfolk, goblins, and other primitives. Long used to eating humanoid flesh, it prefers living offerings, though its service can be bought with gold and adamantine (which it eats to harden its shell).

Brigh

Brigh, the Whisper in the Bronze, is a puzzling goddess of unknown origin, the patron of technologies too complex for most folk to understand. She is the goddess of invention, particularly of devices that seem to possess a life of their own, such as clockwork constructs and golems. She promotes insatiable curiosity, endless experimentation, and the sharing of knowledge, and is responsible for numerous esoteric and expensive creations. As a result, she is popular among gnomes, and many designers, inventors and other brilliant minds capable of comprehending her vision of innovation pray for her blessing. Outside of these few worshipers, however, Brigh remains relatively unknown across the world.

THE WHISPER IN THE BRONZE

Goddess of clockwork, invention, and time

Alignment N

Domains Artifice, Earth, Fire, Knowledge

Subdomains Construct, Metal, Smoke, Thought

Favored Weapon light hammer

Centers of Worship Absalom, Druma, Mana Wastes, Nex, Numeria

Nationality Taldan

Obedience While reciting formulas from *Logic of Design*, you must craft a new creation, continue work on an elaborate device or object, or disassemble an existing creation to see how it works. Favored projects among the church include useful gear, magic items, innovative toys, and contraptions invented primarily to see if they would work rather than to solve a specific problem. Share the knowledge you discover while

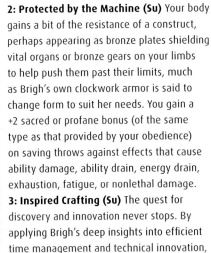

> Need spawns invention, but imagination gives rise to need.
>
> —*Logic of Design*

working on this project. If no people are around to hear or read your observations, or you are incapable of communicating with anyone, instead write down notes about your work to publish or otherwise share with others later. If you can share these notes with someone but choose not to, your obedience is unfulfilled; the requirement to share a set of these notes needs only be met once for that set of notes. You gain a +4 sacred or profane bonus on Disable Device checks. The type of bonus depends on your alignment—if you're neither good nor evil, you must choose either sacred or profane the first time you perform your obedience, and this choice can't be changed.

EVANGELIST BOONS

1: Voice of Bronze (Sp) *jury-rig*^{UC} 3/day, *fox's cunning* 2/day, or *sands of time*^{UM} 1/day

2: Living Construct (Su) The Whisper in the Bronze is the patron of constructs, and through the teachings of her faith, you have learned how to sense the animating spirits within such mechanical entities. You can affect constructs with magic as if they were living creatures. Once per day, you can target a construct with a spell or spell-like ability, and the spell resolves as if the construct's creature type were humanoid. This can bypass intelligent constructs' immunity to mind-affecting effects, but mindless constructs remain unaffected.

3: Time Bounce (Sp) Time is simply a construct, and as such, it can be understood and manipulated. You gain the ability to perceive the flow of time and alter it around yourself, giving you the ability to bounce through time-space from one place to another. Once per day, you

can use *dimensional bounce*^{ACG} as a spell-like ability.

EXALTED BOONS

1: Creator (Sp) *crafter's fortune*^{APG} 3/day, *make whole* 2/day, or *minor creation* 1/day

2: Protected by the Machine (Su) Your body gains a bit of the resistance of a construct, perhaps appearing as bronze plates shielding vital organs or bronze gears on your limbs to help push them past their limits, much as Brigh's own clockwork armor is said to change form to suit her needs. You gain a +2 sacred or profane bonus (of the same type as that provided by your obedience) on saving throws against effects that cause ability damage, ability drain, energy drain, exhaustion, fatigue, or nonlethal damage.

3: Inspired Crafting (Su) The quest for discovery and innovation never stops. By applying Brigh's deep insights into efficient time management and technical innovation, you can craft items in spare moments squeezed in while adventuring or otherwise serving your god's ideals. When crafting magic items while adventuring, you can devote 4 hours each day to creation and take advantage of the full amount of time spent crafting instead of netting only 2 hours' worth of work. In addition, you can use *fabricate* once per day as a spell-like ability. Although you can't create magic items with the *fabricate* spell, you can use it to create items that you later enhance magically.

SENTINEL BOONS

1: Bronze Warrior (Sp) *crafter's curse*^{APG} 3/day, *heat metal* 2/day, or *haste* 1/day

2: Constructed Form (Su) Brigh is fond of adjusting, adding, and removing devices from her internal mechanical workings to constantly improve her design, and she blesses you with a trace of this ability. As a swift action, you can alter your body to incorporate construct-like features that protect you from physical damage. The transformation is subtle, such as adding metal reinforcements along your bones or small, auxiliary clockwork counterparts to your vital organs. The transformation grants you DR 3/— and lasts for a number of rounds per day equal to your Hit Dice. These rounds need not be consecutive. Dismissing the effect is a free action.

3: Call to Battle (Su) Brigh's mechanical servants answer your call to defend inventions, innocent constructs, and the victims of misguided inventions. Once per day as a full-round action, you can summon a clockwork golem (*Pathfinder RPG Bestiary 2* 137). It has the extraplanar subtype but is otherwise a typical golem of its kind. The golem follows your commands perfectly for 1 round per Hit Die you possess before vanishing.

KEEPERS OF CONSTRUCTS

Brigh has tasked her inquisitors with stopping anyone who dares to abuse constructs. They devote special effort to hunting down crafters who infuse objects with intellect, only to treat them as slaves. Other key duties include finding and ending the work of inventors who defile and hurt constructed creatures.

In addition to protecting constructs from people, Brigh's inquisitors also protect people from constructs. When a golem runs amok or a soulbound shell schemes to kidnap those who remind it of its old life, the agents of the Whisper in Bronze strive to stop it. If possible, these inquisitors prefer to contain and repair rampaging constructs, but if necessary, they will destroy these dangerous creations for the long-term benefit of society and invention. Afterward, they always seek to closely study the construct to determine what went wrong in its creation, programming, or maintenance in order to prevent similar problems from befalling other constructs.

UNDERSTANDING BRIGH

Brigh is a patient, calm inventor willing to learn from mistakes and constantly trying to improve her work. Quiet and reserved, she is careful to not offend with casual words or gestures. However, she is not without emotion, and treasures the things her followers craft in her name. There is a special place in her mechanical heart for intelligent constructs, and she punishes anyone who abuses them.

The goddess teaches that people should build upon the work of others and share their own achievements to be improved upon. Creations are to be treated like children, as a legacy of which to be proud. Paying attention to details is critical; one should identify a problem, plot a course of action to correct that problem, and try a different course if the first doesn't work.

Brigh's past is so mysterious that her own priests have several theories regarding her origin. Some preach she was originally a created being that moved beyond the faculties of a normal construct and gained a spark of life and divinity. Others believe she was once a living person, a talented prodigy studying alchemy and clockwork who spent centuries working in isolation. By uniting disparate theories of natural life and construct creation, she was able to seamlessly fuse mechanical parts with her body to attain incredible powers of strength, agility, and mental calculation, eventually perfecting herself into something on the border between mortal and god.

Brigh sometimes manifests as a slender human woman made of bronze clockwork. Other times she appears as a humanoid woman with perfectly symmetrical features wearing clockwork armor (parts of which she can split off and transform into clockwork weapons) and a bronze skullcap. It is unclear which of these is her actual form, or whether both are aspects of her true self. In her clockwork form, Brigh can open a cavity in her chest and draw out perfectly crafted mechanisms she then bestows on other creatures or releases to operate as independent creatures.

When Brigh is pleased, damaged gears spontaneously repair themselves, mirrors acquire a bronze color, constructs whisper words of encouragement, the smell of grease or gunpowder wafts through the air, and worshipers acquire sudden insight into their current projects. When she is angered, alchemical reagents explode, mindless constructs go berserk, intelligent constructs rebel, grease and oil spontaneously catch fire, quills break, inkpots spill, and innocuous materials become irritants.

THE CHURCH

Also known as the Whisper in the Bronze, Brigh communicates with her followers like a mentor or a learned professor, dispensing advice, proofs, and data to push the limits of her audience's understanding and inspire greater and more impressive creations. She is distant even with her own worshipers, as she doesn't like to show favoritism. Many of her worshipers prefer the company of tools and machines to other living beings, however, and thus don't consider this aloofness unusual. Brigh and her church understand physical and emotional needs such as food, sex, and friendship, but think people shouldn't make such base needs their top priorities.

Typical worshipers of Brigh are experts who craft with their hands, especially blacksmiths, gemcutters, jewelers, inventors, and toymakers. Some alchemists more interested in pure research than the practicality of their inventions revere her, and their experimentation yields many novel items, including the occasional useful one. Inventors who pray to her see her as the personification of their art.

The Whisper in the Bronze is a patron of all invention, even destructive devices, for a dangerous tool can still be used for creative purposes. Her church opposes destroying information, which sets back the advancement of technology for everyone. Her priests often seek out and rescue notes, records, and journals that might otherwise be eradicated by fearful enemies of a dangerous inventor. If a person's research leads in a direction believed to be dangerous or immoral, however, that person is free to stop pursuing it. The inventor is then expected to share why he stopped and inform others of potential consequences.

In art, Brigh is typically depicted in her living or her clockwork form, though she is sometimes represented by a bronze mask hovering in place. Gnome artists depict her proportioned like a gnome instead of a human, with long eyebrows and hair made of multicolored metallic wires.

Worship services mix bells, the sounds of music boxes, and the recitation of formulae (such as the inverse relation between gas volume, pressure, and temperature, or the quantities of metals in a salt bath needed to produce electricity). Offerings are made to the goddess during these ceremonies and usually consist of highly refined oils, rare materials, well-used tools, and demonstrations of new inventions.

Brigh has little interest in mortal marriage or families. However, she recognizes that her worshipers may need such things, and that talent for intellect and invention are often inherited, so if a mortal wants to devote energy to such matters, she accepts this. Even offspring with no talent for study can be useful for cleaning work areas, taking dictation, transcribing notes, or performing grunt labor—assuming they are old enough not to endanger themselves or the experiment.

Most of her worshipers are humans, but she also has gnome, half-elven, and half-orc followers. Many intelligent constructs consider her their patron god.

TEMPLES AND SHRINES

There are few temples to Brigh, and most are built like workshops, with places for crafting and tinkering. Many include a shop selling items crafted by the temple, or warehouse space for items destined to be sent elsewhere. The head of a temple is called the High Clockmother or High Clockfather, and is usually the most knowledgeable priest at that location, if not the most powerful. The luckiest priests have sponsors who provide funds and supplies, allowing them to devote all their time to their work; many temples accept donations for this purpose or sell useful items to fund their resident priests. Some temples craft a clockwork shell in Brigh's likeness and use it as an object of veneration. One of the largest temples to Brigh is in Alkenstar.

Shrines to Brigh are much more common than temples, and many workshops and laboratories have a bronze mask or large gear mounted on the wall to honor her. Successful inventors who feel they owe inspiration or their foundational knowledge to Brigh often leave offerings to her at such altars. Less often, unsuccessful and disheartened inventors who give up on their work leave dysfunctional devices at these shrines in the hope that the more learned faithful might find a way to perfect them.

A PRIEST'S ROLE

Priests are expected to devote much of their lives to research. For most, this means experimenting and inventing in a workshop or laboratory. A few priests pursue interests that require fieldwork or exploration, followed by time in a settlement where they refine their experimental methodology or expand their notes into monographs that can then be shared with other researchers.

Other priests of Brigh become peddlers or tinkerers, selling their inventions or those created by others and spreading the word about how these devices can make life easier, more efficient, or more entertaining. Brigh's priests loathe quacks, charlatans, and sellers of fraudulent goods—though some peddler-priests of the Whisper in the Bronze sell controversial items to armies, thieves' guilds, and tyrants. They may create subtle traps for doors, more powerful (and expensive) variants of crossbows or firearms, clockwork spies, or crank-powered electrical torture devices.

Brigh's clerics are usually trained in Craft (alchemy, carpentry, clocks, glass, leather, or locks), Knowledge (engineering), and Profession (architect, engineer, miner, or scribe). Those who perform dangerous research train in the Heal skill as well, in case something goes wrong. Adventuring clerics usually have ranks in Craft (weapons) or Disable Device.

Because their interests are so specialized, priests of Brigh usually don't have active roles in their communities. The exceptions are in Alkenstar, where the clergy are heavily involved in the development and manufacture of firearms, and Numeria, where they catalog artifacts scavenged from the surrounding lands. Brigh's faith is so small that outside of those two technology-minded lands, few people have even heard of her, and fewer still have met one of her priests. Most priests have no interest in proselytizing, and many avoid discussing religion with layfolk.

Each morning, a priest typically rises, eats a simple and efficient meal, and refreshes her mind in preparation for the day's work. Many are so driven that they work long hours and forget to eat or sleep, and must be reminded to do so

by a spouse, assistant, or timepiece. The use of stimulants to increase productivity or waking hours is common. Priests are used to erratic schedules and may become frustrated by others who prefer a more traditional routine. More practical folk say these inventors are "married to the Whisper," in much the way that new lovers are so obsessed with each other that they forget all else. Those who work in a group environment (such as a temple-funded workshop) are used to consulting with others about problems, and long, enthusiastic talks between colleagues often contribute to the late hours. Those who have larger roles in their communities might work on projects such as better ballistae to protect the town, more efficient ways to stabilize mine tunnels, or experimental clinics offering free (and potentially unorthodox) healing.

Brigh's priests are primarily clerics, although the church also includes a few inquisitors. Her clerics can prepare *unbreakable construct*UM as a 5th-level spell and *control construct*UM as a 7th-level spell.

ADVENTURERS

Devout adventurers serving Brigh usually see adventuring as a way to come into contact with new ideas and record that knowledge for posterity. Most operate like priests undertaking field research. They might include searching the records of old civilizations for hints about their metallurgy techniques or lost technology, looking for higher-quality sources of alchemical materials, or taking advantage of natural phenomena that can't easily be reproduced by mortal hands (such as unusual magnetism, pockets of magma, or frequent lightning strikes). They take side treks to see new inventions or contact noteworthy thinkers, and offer their services to inventors.

Adventuring worshipers of Brigh are known for keeping detailed journals tracking their observations about the world or ideas for ways to make work easier or accomplish new things. Most carry an astounding variety of adventuring gear and wondrous items. New and strange forms of equipment, alchemical items, and weapons like firearms quickly draw their attention.

CLOTHING

There is no formal dress for the clergy, but many wear a leather work coat accented with bronze buttons and clasps for both work and worship. Somewhere on the coat is usually a large button or brooch in the shape of Brigh's mask. A pair of oversized leather-bound goggles and a close-fitting leather cap, which double as protective laboratory gear, complete the outfit, which acquires a respectable assortment of scorch marks, acid burns, and patched areas over time. A priest might add a decorative badge showing her field of interest or indicating a significant invention or accolade given to her by other inventors for her contributions to technological progress.

Worshipers often wear a toothed gear as jewelry, and some carry sets of miniature tools as ritual objects when full-sized versions would be unnecessary or impractical. Adventurers who serve Brigh often wear helmets in the shape of her holy mask, decorated with bronze accents.

HOLY TEXT

Very little of Brigh's texts are presented as religious dogma; instead, they are framed as information established through research and study.

Logic of Design: The official book of the church is presented as an essay, or perhaps the transcription of a lecture, covering the basic ideas of innovation, experimentation, documentation, and discovery. Later sections provide a cursory overview of the fields of metallurgy, electricity, physics (particularly in relation to motion), and stonemasonry, as if the book were intended to be a primer for a series of university courses instead of a holy text. Large parts of these later sections have a different writing style than the first part, as if fleshed out by students or other researchers.

HOLIDAYS

Brigh has no set holidays, though individual temples make note of the anniversaries of important discoveries and inventions, particularly if they are tied to that community. These remembrances take place at a convenient time within a few days of the event's actual anniversary. Temples usually give a nod to local holidays and those of friendly divinities if the holidays have some aspect that's of interest to the church.

Sunwrought Festival: Brigh's followers often help celebrate Sarenrae's holiday by crafting fireworks.

Taxfest: Brigh's faithful celebrate Abadar's Taxfest by performing complex calculations to make sure there is no inaccuracy in the taxes they owe.

Wrights of Augustana: The church in Andoran takes this day to praise the math and engineering necessary to build large ships.

APHORISMS

As Brigh's followers are always struggling to expand the frontiers of knowledge, many of the faith's common phrases are meant to inspire hope and determination.

Invention Is Immortality: For the many followers of Brigh so devoted to their craft that they cannot maintain a family and never have children, their inventions are their children and their work is their legacy. Allowing others to learn and use their discoveries is at least as good as passing on a family name.

Question, Propose, Test: The basis of understanding the world is to think of a question, propose an answer to it, and find a way to test whether or not that answer is true. Each of these concepts is part of a "perfect triangle" of understanding; all three parts are necessary and interdependent. Questioning without proposals or testing is mere philosophy. An answer can't exist without a question, and an answer without testing is mere speculation. Testing without a question or hypothesis is dangerous experimentation.

Share What You Know: Every discovery since the dawn of civilization has allowed later inventors to create even greater things than those who came before them. Refusing to at least share documentation posthumously is like stealing from starving future minds.

RELATIONS WITH OTHER RELIGIONS

Brigh is careful not to antagonize other gods or get in the middle of feuds. Of the major deities, she is closest with Shelyn, despite having few common interests aside from a focus on artistic creation. Brigh and Desna are fond of each other, as they share a wonder for discovery. She is also close with Abadar, who admires the fruits of her invention—particularly items that improve construction methods, allow for faster counting and calculation, and facilitate record-keeping. She looks favorably on Torag because of his focus on creation and work with the forge, but he is ambivalent toward her because of her apathy toward families. Brigh is on good terms with Cayden Cailean, who appreciates the science behind brewing. She and Norgorber have collaborated in the past on certain aspects of alchemical research, though his unwillingness to share information has soured this relationship. Brigh has a close working relationship with other nonevil gods who share the Artifice domain, particularly the empyreal lords Bharnarol and Eldas.

Although some of her followers' inventions prove useful and interesting to followers of Gorum, they are fundamentally beside the point to the god of war, who gives weapon inventors little regard. Brigh detests Rovagug, as there is no creation in him, only destruction. She avoids dealing with evil gods who cannot be reasoned with, which generally means most of them aside from Asmodeus.

Regardless of Brigh's opinions regarding the other gods, she makes no rules regarding with whom her worshipers can associate, as the free pursuit of new knowledge can lead to strange but ultimately beneficial partnerships. Her priests' obsession with knowledge and its pursuit does produce some hostilities, however. Priests of Asmodeus and Zon-Kuthon see the free exchange of ideas as a threat to their hegemonic influence over Cheliax and Nidal, respectively.

Norgorber's faithful have repeatedly sent agents to silence inconvenient alchemical and healing researchers. As a result, Brigh's clergy often avoid discussing religion around followers of those faiths, pretending to be irreligious or nominal followers of more popular gods.

REALM

Brigh's realm, the Citadel of Resplendent Clockwork, is located in Axis. The structure is a vast, labyrinthine machine of moving cogs, shimmering colored glass, and spinning flywheels, constantly reconfiguring itself to suit its mistress's current interests. Within, Brigh has secured the assistance of some secretive inevitables as part of an ongoing collaboration with the axiomites.

PLANAR ALLIES

Many of Brigh's divine servants were once mortal inventors, but have been recreated in "perfect" mechanical forms; she treats them as her children or younger siblings. Her following servitors are the ones most likely to respond to *planar ally*.

Karapek (unique human alchemist): This dark-haired man is made of bronze, and has large hands and a back reinforced with struts of polished steel. He is knowledgeable regarding constructs and flesh golem construction, and sees himself as an ambassador between living creatures and sentient constructs.

Latten Mechanism (herald of Brigh): Brigh's herald (*Pathfinder Adventure Path* #86 84) is a defender of constructs and crafters, a living siege engine who prefers the solitude of research to the distractions of battle. It has a massive insectile form, and its only humanlike feature is the androgynous face built into the top of its insectile head. Able to tear open castle gates, scoop up enemies and crush them in its body, and form walls or complex objects out of raw materials or thin air, Latten Mechanism is a versatile engine of both creation and destruction guided by its mechanical conscience. It has a childlike appreciation for small but cleverly constructed clockwork objects, such as music boxes and hopping animals.

Dahak

Dahak, the Endless Destruction, is ancient beyond measure. The first child of the primordial draconic deities Apsu and Tiamat, Dahak turned against Apsu out of jealousy when he saw his father shower his siblings with attention and affection. He rampaged throughout the multiverse, murdering his siblings, only to reforge them into mortals on the Material Plane, where he tormented them further. The extent of his destruction secured his place as the embodiment of savage ruin. Now, Dahak is the patron of a wicked flock. He and his followers wreak havoc wherever they roam, endlessly striving to obliterate all that is good and uplifting across reality in preparation for a final battle with Apsu.

THE ENDLESS DESTRUCTION

God of destruction, evil dragons, and greed

Alignment CE

Domains Chaos, Destruction, Evil, Scalykind, Trickery

Subdomains Catastrophe, Deception, Demon, Dragon, Rage, Thievery

Favored Weapon bite or whip

Centers of Worship Darklands, the Shackles, Thuvia

Nationality dragon

Obedience Remain entirely silent for 1 hour while you pray to Dahak, ruminating over the glories of wanton destruction committed as the culmination of waiting and planning. While you pray, let hate and anger fill you until you must lash out. Following your prayer, destroy an item worth at least 1 gp and use the shattered remains to cut yourself, preferably along preexisting scar lines, while espousing your love of chaos and destruction. Such an action deals you 1 point of damage that cannot be healed for the following 24 hours. You gain a +2 profane bonus on Bluff and Intimidate checks against creatures who can see your scars.

EVANGELIST BOONS

1: Sorrowmaker's Pact (Sp) *protection from good* 3/day, *align weapon* (evil only) 2/day, or *rage* 1/day

2: Enemy of Dragonkind (Su) You can protect yourself from the noble forces of the universe and are attuned to blocking out draconic threats. When you are under the effects of *protection from good* or a similar effect, true dragons with fewer Hit Dice than you count as summoned creatures for the purpose of interacting with you, regardless of their alignment. In addition, three times per day while under such an effect, you can reroll one saving throw against a breath weapon, spell, or spell-like ability used against you by a creature of the dragon type. You can only reroll a single saving throw once.

3: Bow Before Your End! (Su) You represent one of the most powerful deities in the cosmos, and you expect all creatures to recognize the unspeakable power you herald and its capacity for wanton destruction. Once per day as a standard action, you can create an effect similar to *overwhelming presence*[UM] as though you were a cleric with an effective caster level equal to half your Hit Dice. Creatures that fail their saving throws are staggered instead of helpless for the duration of the spell, and suffer no further effects upon a successful subsequent save. Creatures of the dragon type must roll their saving throws twice and take the lower result. A creature that

succeeds at its initial saving throw is unaffected by this effect.

EXALTED BOONS

1: Rites of the False Wyrm (Sp) *charm person* 3/day, *mirror image* 2/day, or *suggestion* 1/day.

2: Draconic Decoys (Su) Duplicity is second nature to you, and you know how to manipulate trickery-based magic to further confound your enemies. Anytime you have created an image via *mirror image*, as a swift action you can direct one of your images to move to a flanking position against an enemy within 15 feet of you. The image allows you or an ally to flank your target for the purpose of a single attack. A redirected image dissipates when you or an ally uses the image to make a flanking attack, or otherwise remains in place for 1 round before dissipating.

3: Flaming Vengeance (Su) You believe that if your enemies are foolish enough to trust you, then they are foolish enough to die by Dahak's power. Once per day as a standard action, you can gain the benefits of a *mislead* spell as though cast by a wizard of a level equal to your Hit Dice (maximum 20th level), with the following modifications. At the time of using this ability, you can establish a number of rounds before it will expire, or declare that it will expire when your illusory duplicate is touched. When either criteria is accomplished, the illusory duplicate explodes as a *fireball* spell cast by a 10th-level wizard.

SENTINEL BOONS

1: Power of the Endless Destruction (Sp) *ear-piercing scream*[UM] 3/day, *shatter* 2/day, or *fireball* 1/day

2: Teeth of the Dragon (Ex) Your teeth grow into vicious fangs, akin to those of a chromatic dragon, and elemental power issues forth from your mouth in a divine gift from Dahak himself. You gain a bite attack. This is a primary natural attack that deals 1d6 points of piercing damage for Medium creatures or 1d4 points of piercing damage for Small creatures, with a critical multiplier of ×3. Every time you hit with your bite attack, you deal an additional 1d6 points of energy damage (choose from acid, cold, electricity, or fire).

3: Elemental Outrage (Ex) You can channel the power of the Endless Destruction through your vicious bites—when you hit a creature with your bite attack, you can force impressive elemental power into the attack. Up to three times per day, when you succeed at a critical hit with your bite attack, you deal 5d6 points of energy damage (choose from acid, cold, electricity, or fire) instead of 1d6 points. This extra damage is not multiplied as part of the critical hit.

> So comes the time when the sky burns, and great wings unfold. So comes the time when all our prayers are answered, and all things are rendered to ash.
>
> —The Pyre of Dahak

DAHAK'S ANTIPALADIN CODE

Antipaladins of Dahak are grim servants of the Endless Destruction, their demeanor calm up until the moment their control slips. They hunt metallic dragons as a means of repaying Dahak for his blessing. Dahak lays down several tenets for his divine warriors to follow.

- I am an instrument of destruction, but the power I wield is mine to control, gifted to me by Dahak.
- My wrath is ceaseless. It is by my judgment alone to decide when I shall unleash it. Once I strike an enemy, I will not stop until they are dead.
- None are safe from the rage that boils within me. While some may be spared immediate death, I offer no such lenience to the metallic dragons, greatest of enemies to the power that gives me strength.
- Forgiveness is for the weak. If I am slighted, I will go to any lengths to enact my vengeance.

UNDERSTANDING DAHAK

Left to fend for himself after his birth, Dahak roamed the fields of primeval Hell. He eventually emerged and came into contact with his siblings—the numerous draconic divinities living under Apsu's guiding talons. Irrational rage filled Dahak at the prosperity and friendship those deities shared, and so he shattered each of them in turn. He then ensured that they returned as mortals to be tormented again. Each of the broken deities filled the Material Plane with countless draconic progeny, which became the first metallic dragons.

Apsu eventually confronted his wayward son and found that Dahak hunted the metallic dragons for sport. Father and son warred in a terrifying aerial battle, flying between worlds, with Dahak slowly gaining the upper hand. Only the metallic dragons' intervention turned the tide, and Apsu wrestled Dahak to the surface of the Material Plane and irrevocably scarred the raging dragon. But before Apsu could strike the final blow, Tiamat intervened, saving her son and betraying the noble Apsu. Dahak escaped, along with the first chromatic dragons—creatures reformed through Tiamat's blessing from the dying metallic dragons that littered the battlefield.

Dahak withdrew, keen to let his wounds heal. He eventually learned of his father's creation of the roaming demiplane realm known as the Immortal Ambulatory. The Endless Destruction prepared to siege his father's realm in a decisive battle. But Apsu's attention suddenly turned to Golarion, joining the greater deific pantheon battling the ravening god Rovagug, and so Dahak followed.

The evil dragon knew Apsu would be present and engaged in the battle himself, intending to betray his father at a key moment in the apocalyptic struggle.

Instead, some part of Dahak recognized the universal threat the Rough Beast presented, and so he fully committed to the effort to imprison Rovagug. As the dust of the conflict settled, Apsu spoke with his son; he told Dahak that he had expected betrayal, and was surprised it had not manifested. Dahak vowed then to kill his father, and Apsu declared that Golarion would be their final battlefield. If Dahak ever returns to the world to wreak his destruction—potentially weakening the bonds that hold Rovagug—Apsu has pledged to stop him.

THE CHURCH

Few willingly serve in what constitutes Dahak's church, as most who learn of the Endless Destruction are revolted by what he represents. The dictates of Dahak require the application of overwhelming force to defeat one's enemies. These beliefs differ from Rovagug's uncontrolled raging, as Dahak is capable of periods of civility and discussion. He often broods during such times—right up until he undertakes a violent rampage. The church of Dahak is similar, especially on Golarion where it is currently engaged in a "civil" phase. Dahak's Golarion-based clergy will turn on others only when their enemies have sufficiently aggravated them, or Dahak's own divine messages shift fully toward destruction.

One of Dahak's greatest champions on Golarion is **Aashaq the Annihilator** (CE female great wyrm red dragon cleric of Dahak 7). She is a powerful red dragon who shuns all her draconic kin save those who serve her. Residing on the island of Dahak's Fang within the Shackles, Aashaq has carved a path of destruction throughout the pirate-dominated region. Now Dahak's Fang and a collection of surrounding islands called Dahak's Teeth are home to Aashaq's dragon underlings, each vying for prominence in the red dragon's growing congregation.

Enclaves of Dahak-worshiping humans also secretly meet in Thuvia, particularly in the settlement of Pashow. These faithful of the Endless Destruction work alongside the servants of the demigod Ahriman, seeking to entice the Lord of All Divs to leave Abaddon and enter Golarion through the nearby House of Oblivion.

Many of the disparate kobold tribes residing below the earth, in subterranean sewers and some regions of Nar-Voth, venerate Dahak. These tribes connect with their religion through one or more dragon speakers—kobolds whom Dahak blesses with nightmares. Such divinely touched kobolds work within their tribes to promote the great Dahak, speaking of the countless creation myths that surround him and the kobold race as a whole. The lifestyle of a kobold is fitting for servants of Dahak, who often work for long stretches of clarity and purpose, only to explode in bursts of rage and bloodletting.

Beyond Golarion, worship of Dahak is common on Triaxus, as is that of Apsu, and the two faiths' adherents often find themselves coming into conflict—particularly when dragons and dragonkin are concerned.

TEMPLES AND SHRINES

Dahak is as vain a creature as any chromatic dragon and heartily approves of places of worship erected in his name. Such sites are predominantly in hidden places, away from the prying eyes of Apsu's noble followers or other equally altruistic deities such as Iomedae or Sarenrae. The majority of Dahak's temples are found in subterranean caves or in secret complexes beneath cities. Smaller sites of worship are often the purview of lone chromatic dragons defying others of their kind to seek Dahak's blessing, or crafted by tribes of kobolds who see Dahak as part of their creation myth. Powerful dragons typically maintain the larger sites, though humanoids sometimes clandestinely craft vast cathedrals to the Endless Destruction under their cities' streets.

Dahak's few temples are almost always crafted from well-worked stone and are majestically cyclopean sites. These temples are designed to awe visitors and accommodate creatures the size of massive dragons. Illusion magic powers these temples' lights, which usually resemble the blazing breath weapons of chromatic dragons held within jagged stone cages.

A PRIEST'S ROLE

Other than the obediences performed by the most faithful, a devotee of Dahak is not expected to follow a given routine, or to perform daily deference to the deity. The true calling of Dahak's devoted is to serve their master's role in preparing Golarion as the battleground for the fateful final combat between Dahak and his father. Even worshipers far removed from Golarion can contribute to this goal, the best method being to hunt down metallic dragons. By performing these purges, Dahak's followers ensure that Apsu's strength will be weakened come their eventual battle.

On Golarion, Dahak communicates primarily with his faithful through powerful nightmarish visions. Such touched servants catch glimpses of the endless rage beneath Dahak's falsely calm surface and can relay their god's words to others following their creed. The veracity of such visions is often debated, and many times requires a supposed prophet to prove he has Dahak's blessing by performing a task or by demonstrating the benediction of the Endless Destruction. Those gifted with these visions must continually contend with other members of their church, even when the facts revealed are indisputable, lest the visionaries find themselves betrayed at the hands of a new prophet.

Dahak's priests have little interaction with the countless humanoid civilizations of the Material Plane, save for the missions of their god. In cases where Dahak's will is not evident, priests seek out those they believe may have a connection with their god. In many cases, such priests end up at the feet of a great chromatic dragon only to find out that the dragon has no connection with Dahak—in fact, many chromatic dragons oppose the Endless Destruction

and slay those foolish enough to utter his name in their presence. Another misconception about Dahak's faithful is that they actively pursue Apsu's agents. In truth, while the clergy of Apsu is righteously dedicated to expunging Dahak's servants, adherents of the Endless Destruction have no similar drive, other than to slay those metallic dragons in service to Apsu. Furthermore, Dahak often guides his children away from attacking the non-draconic followers of Apsu, for he wishes to slay each of them personally on the eve of his final battle with his father.

Among Dahak's worshipers, half-dragon adherents receive the highest esteem, especially if they are of chromatic descent. The chromatic dragons' large-scale abandonment of Dahak was a serious blow to the Endless Destruction's martial power, so loyal servitors (even of mixed parentage) are seen as divine apostles in most churches of Dahak. Other draconically inclined creatures, such as drakes, dragonkin, kobolds, and even humanoids with levels in the dragon disciple prestige class, are thought of as valuable or symbolic tools, as long as they willingly serve Dahak's destructive needs.

ADVENTURERS

Dragons, kobolds, and half-dragons are the creatures most likely to willingly worship Dahak without joining an official religious order. Preferred class levels include barbarian, bloodrager, ranger, sorcerer, and warpriest. Such followers of Dahak can be civil up until the point of combat, whereupon they erupt in a flurry of destructive rage against their enemies. Adventurers serving Dahak differ from the nihilistic followers of Rovagug in the simple fact that they can maintain self-control, and usually only unleash their anger when faced with people or situations that provoke their ire them.

Kobolds are the only race whose common folk have any accepted devotion to Dahak; several of their tribes believe that the Endless Destruction is a key part of their genesis. Among other humanoids, knowledge of Dahak is so scarce that few even know the name, and those that happen upon a text detailing the Sorrowmaker often have little reason to venerate such a power.

CLOTHING

Outsiders believe the favored color of Dahak to be black, when in fact his followers wear numerous chromatic vestments. Among adherents, black and red are staple colors simply because clothes and armor are often stained black by fire or red by carnage. Priests able to properly clean their attire present themselves in robes of varying colors, with blue, green, and red being dominant. Those among dragon families and kobold tribes often use the coloration of robes to denote rank; typically, the natural color of the specific draconic species is the highest rank.

HOLY TEXT

Upon hearing of the penning of the *Draconic Apsu* by the esteemed gold dragon sage Gunnarrex, Dahak wished for a similar treatise to distribute to his servants. Gunnarrex was yanked into Dahak's realm, where the Endless Destruction tortured him into penning *The Pyre of Dahak*. Detailing a ruinous future promised to Apsu and his metallic dragon progeny, the religious text has made its way through the Material Plane and the Great Beyond. Dahak's livid discourse scarred the dragon sage's mind and soul; after penning the document, Gunnarrex tore out his eyes and declared himself an atheist.

HOLIDAYS

Dahak's followers are not a sentimental lot, but they typically recognize two major holidays.

Day of Amends: Once per year, on a date of their choosing, Dahak's followers try to coax a chromatic dragon into returning to the worship of the Endless Destruction. Such attempts are often met with gruesome deaths.

The Release: Occurring once every millennia on the date Dahak is said to have first fought Apsu, this event provides an opportunity for Dahak's followers to sate their pent-up bloodlust, turning on those around them in a day of unending ruin. Many scholars speculate that the next Release soon approaches.

APHORISMS

The following sayings are common among Dahak's followers and mirror the destructive deity's primal ways.

I Am Descended of Tiamat: Attributed to Dahak during his first battle with Apsu, this line is spoken by the Endless Destruction's modern servants to boast of their connection to the primordial dragon mother. Speaking these words refer to the powers that created Dahak and acts as a battle cry for those entering combat—particularly against the servants of Apsu.

My Patience Is Like Fire: Many deities have noted Dahak's capacity for civility, despite his moniker of the Endless Destruction. Dahak's followers use this aphorism to warn others not to unduly test their tolerance.

RELATIONS WITH OTHER RELIGIONS

Most deities prefer to keep their distance from Dahak. Asmodeus, however, is cordial with him, having dealt with Dahak in the days when the dragon god flew over the primordial landscape of Hell. Rumors hold that the Dark Prince has made several proposals of a partnership to Dahak, offering to weaken the Endless Destruction's father before their final conflict in exchange for some unknown favor. Other whispers tell of the Asmodeus conducting similar negotiations Apsu, making the Lord of the Pit's actual intentions doubly unclear

Calistria is said to bear at least one hidden scar from her attempts to court Dahak. Now, the elven goddess warns her followers to be wary of Dahak's servants, while also encouraging them to manipulate the Endless Destruction's followers into acts of vengeance when merciless destruction is necessary.

Dahak's greatest enemy is his father, Apsu. The two draconic gods have battled throughout history, only having ever fought side by side once, in the skies of Golarion, when they helped to imprison the Rough Beast. Despite the clarity of purpose Dahak showed in helping the other gods in this venture, he has no plans to ever work alongside his father again—in fact, Dahak's entire existence is now focused on preparing for his final confrontation with Apsu.

The archdevil Mephistopheles has a longstanding relationship with Dahak, having ceded territory within his home of Caina to serve as the evil god's realm. Dahak eagerly took the archdevil's offer, building a sanctuary in which he could recover his strength. In exchange for this boon, Dahak crafted the quill of Caina's lord, the artifact *Visineir*, from the heart of an adamantine mountain in the upper reaches of Nessus. Despite this, Mephistopheles holds no contract or binding oath with Dahak. The devils of Hell's lowest regions whisper of Asmodeus's direct involvement in this arrangement, some believing the lord of Hell and Mephistopheles came to an agreement to ensure Dahak's continued existence for some nefarious purpose.

REALM

The Adamantine Morass is Dahak's realm, a web of tunnels stretching throughout the lowest depths of Caina, Hell's eighth layer. The winding paths begin as a maze of dirt and stone tunnels, and end in a series of warrens leading into a realm of adamantine. Here, Dahak stalks those foolish enough to enter his realm uninvited, enjoying the thrill of the chase through the lightless, twisting tunnels. Those unable to provide the Endless Destruction with enough enjoyment through their chase are instead cast into the *Well of Venoms*, a caustic blend of acid and hellfire said to be capable of shattering an *Orb of Dragonkind*.

PLANAR ALLIES

Despite his fickle nature, Dahak's planar alliances stretch back almost to the beginning of his existence. The following creatures can be summoned using spells such as *planar ally*.

Emissary Rixmar (unique contract devil): This always-smiling contract devil (*Pathfinder RPG Bestiary 3* 76) walks with the assistance of a great tridentlike quill crafted from one of Dahak's teeth. Rixmar's legs were shattered for disappointing his previous patron—the archdevil Mephistopheles. Now, he serves as Dahak's favored emissary, a sociable enough creature when such skills are required. What brought Rixmar into the service of Dahak is obvious: the contract devil has an incredible temper, ignoring the terms of the contracts he makes if those he deals with sufficiently anger him.

Kronoroth (herald of Dahak): The unique ancient white dragon mercilessly hunts metallic dragons. As Dahak's herald, she accepts only the summons of mortals who promise to let her slay metallic dragons or metallic half-dragons. Her back is lined with spines of black ice, each of which impales the preserved head of a young metallic dragon. Each head allows her to inflict a different torment on her foes. If killed, such creatures rise as ice golems under Kronoroth's command.

The Roiling Mass (unique Medium magma elemental): This magma elemental (*Pathfinder RPG Bestiary 2* 118) is little more than a sentient pool of lava. The Roiling Mass is said to have been created when Dahak's rage was so great that it imparted the fiery residue of his breath weapon with a modicum of self-awareness. The mass has little intelligence, and is summoned only to unleash immediate and rampant destruction as it consumes all in its oozing path. Those caught and melted alive in its wake can later be seen as rough body features pushing out from within the Roiling Mass.

Ghlaunder

Ghlaunder's will manifests in many ways: the death rattle of an old man's cough, the stench of a stagnant marsh, or the squirming of parasitic worms beneath a child's skin. He prospers wherever disease and decay flourish. The goddess Desna unintentionally unleashed the Gossamer King into the world. Curious about the strange undulations of a silken cocoon on the Ethereal Plane, she sliced it open, and Ghlaunder buzzed forth fully formed. He feasted on the Starsoul's divine blood, and then escaped before Desna could destroy him. And thus the hunt continues through the millennia, with the wily Ghlaunder eluding the goddess at every step while sowing plague, death, and disease.

THE GOSSAMER KING

God of infection, parasites, and stagnation

Alignment CE

Domains Air, Animal, Chaos, Destruction, Evil

Subdomains Catastrophe, Cloud, Demon, Fur, Rage, Wind

Favored Weapon spear

Centers of Worship Mwangi Expanse, Sodden Lands, Varisia

Nationality monster

Obedience Craft a small poppet in the shape of a flea, tick, stirge, or other such plague-carrying creature, using natural materials such as straw, and mixing your blood with foul-smelling mud or dung to bind the poppet together. As it dries over the course of an hour, recite verses invoking virulence, filth, and affliction on the living while applying leeches to your flesh. At the end of the hour, burn the poppet and the leeches, inhaling the foul vapors while meditating on the purging effects of disease on the living while your leech-drawn blood burns in sacrifice to Ghlaunder. If you are affected by a disease, any ability score damage or drain you would take from that disease today is halved; if you would take 1 point of ability score damage, you instead take none. You can still contract diseases and spread them to others as normal.

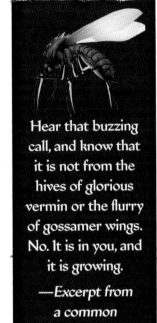

Hear that buzzing call, and know that it is not from the hives of glorious vermin or the flurry of gossamer wings. No. It is in you, and it is growing.

—Excerpt from a common Ghlaunderite ritual

EVANGELIST BOONS

1: Cult of Contagion (Sp) *ray of sickening*UM 3/day, *pox pustules*APG 2/day, or *contagion* 1/day

2: Nauseating Strike (Ex) You know how to use others' capacity for revulsion as a weapon against them. Three times per day, you can make a nauseating strike against an opponent through your weapon, causing the target to feel the effects of a sickening disease. You must declare your use of this ability before you roll your attack, and if your attack misses, the strike is wasted. On a hit, your target must succeed at a Fortitude save (DC = 10 + 1/2 your Hit Dice) or be nauseated for 1d4 rounds, in addition to the normal weapon damage.

3: Debilitating Blight (Sp) Once per day, you can cast *greater contagion*UM as a spell-like ability, infecting the target with a virulent and debilitating disease that takes effect immediately; the DC to resist this disease is 4 higher than normal. In addition to the effects of the disease, the subject is debilitated with wracking coughs and painful, bursting pustules. The incessant sickness imposes a −2 penalty on the target's attack rolls, weapon damage rolls, saving throws, skill checks, and ability modifiers for a number of rounds equal to your Hit Dice.

EXALTED BOONS

1: Infectious Blighter (Sp) *inflict light wounds* 3/day, *accelerate poison*APG 2/day, or *nauseating trail*ACG 1/day

2: Blighting Channel (Su) You bring the desolation of drought and blight to the landscapes through which you pass. Three times per day when you channel negative energy, you can choose to cause damage to plants and plant creatures instead of healing undead. Creatures with the plant type within range take 1d6 points of damage plus 1d6 additional points for every 2 cleric levels beyond 1st you have (maximum 10d6 at 19th level), and can attempt a Fortitude saving throw (using the same DC as for your regular uses of channel negative energy) for half damage. All normal plants in range immediately wither and die (no saving throw).

3: Polluted Servant (Sp) Ghlaunder gifts his most devoted with servants of living filth that fight on the supplicants' behalf to sow death and disease. Once per day as a standard action, you can summon a hezrou demon (*Pathfinder RPG Bestiary* 62) to serve you. The demon follows your commands for 1 round for every Hit Die you have before vanishing back to its home. It doesn't obey commands that would make it perform overtly good acts, and if such instructions are particularly egregious, they could prompt the demon to attack you.

SENTINEL BOONS

1: Poisonous Penitent (Sp) *nauseating dart*ACG 3/day, *pernicious poison*UM 2/day, or *poison* 1/day

2: Bloodletter (Ex) You have trained extensively with Ghlaunder's favored weapon in order to cause severe trauma to your enemies, opening their veins so their blood might spill forth as an offering to your god. You gain a +1 profane bonus on all attack and damage rolls with a spear. In addition, when you confirm a critical hit, your target takes 1 point of bleed damage for every 2 character levels you have. Bleeding creatures take that amount of damage every round at the start of their turns. The bleeding can be stopped with a successful DC 15 Heal check or the application of any effect that heals hit point damage. Bleed damage from this ability or any other effect does not stack with itself. Bleed damage bypasses any damage reduction the creature might have.

3: Horrible Blow (Sp) Once per day, you can inflict a debilitating disease upon your target through your weapon. You must declare your use of this ability before you roll your attack. On a hit, the target is affected as if the subject of *horrid wilting* cast by a wizard of a level equal to your Hit Dice (maximum CL 20th), as well as normal weapon damage. If you miss with your attack, the use of this ability is wasted.

GHLAUNDER AND DESNA

The rivalry between Desna and Ghlaunder is now legendary. Responsible for releasing the demigod upon the world, Desna has struggled for untold eons to capture the Gossamer King and either imprison him again or turn his destructive tendencies toward some higher purpose. But like the hungry mosquito that constantly vexes its target, Ghlaunder forever confounds the Tender of Dreams as he continues to spread filth with every flutter of his diseased wings.

This rivalry extends to the followers of the two, and Ghlaunder's servants revel in infiltrating Desna's clergy. Many are the tales of isolated communities settled by itinerant priests proselytizing the wonders of Desna, only to be rediscovered generations later with its citizens faithfully observing grossly distorted and obscene venerations to a deity that resembles Desna only in causal observation, but whose rites and traditions are actually hijacked supplications to the Gossamer King. In less remote areas where such deceptions may be recognized, Ghlaunder's cultists instead infiltrate the clergy of established temples to leech off their tithing, while using their assumed identities to secretly spoil food, taint wells, and spread sickness until a community is firmly in the grip of plague and parasites.

UNDERSTANDING GHLAUNDER

The Gossamer King rejoices in spreading filth and decay, and his goal is nothing short of an incurable plague that infects all living things. Ghlaunder does not seek the world's destruction—indeed, without the living, contagion cannot take root, parasites cannot thrive, and diseases cannot proliferate. Instead, Ghlaunder revels in the world's sickness, and his followers infest communities as surely as any parasite, often in the guise of devout priests of other religions, while working to cultivate filth and fever. His cultists are indiscriminate in their targets—young, old, fit, or frail, it matters not—so long as they pass their affliction on to the next, then they to another, and like the candle held too close to the curtain, the world alights in infection and death.

Ghlaunder takes the form of a bloated mosquito with a barbed proboscis, his engorged abdomen swollen with alien parasites. His home is a great swamp in the Abyss, a quagmire where the backwaters of the Styx spread into a great sludge of marsh. The mothers of dying infants or the infirm often appeal to Ghlaunder, and the god sometimes grants respite from sickness. But woe are the gifts of the Gossamer King, for those who fight off their infections often wake from their fevered dreams to find their own lives were spared, while they were responsible for the contagion and resulting deaths of their closest loved ones. Ghlaunder's favored weapon is the spear, representing the god's blood-draining proboscis, and his unholy symbol is a blood-engorged mosquito in profile.

THE CHURCH

Ghlaunder's church is unorganized, with myriad splinter faiths, lone priests, and nefarious congregations working independently to accomplish their god's will. Some priests wander from city to city serving Ghlaunder directly, concealing bursting pustules beneath lice-infested robes and spreading diseases to all they come into contact with. Cults of worshipers lurk in the sewers beneath cities where filth accumulates, emerging only to bring the coagulated germs of civilization back to the surface.

In Varisia, Ghlaunder's worship is subtly embedded in the area's cultures. While many cities certainly harbor cults of the mosquito god, the prying eyes of good-aligned deities and the hostility of their mortal emissaries makes the open worship of the Gossamer King a dangerous prospect, even in isolated communities where something as little as a visiting priest can call forth a purge from powerful churches. Ghlaunder's devout who persist in these places have learned their god's lessons best.

In such areas, Ghlaunder's emissaries subvert the religions of more respected deities—Desna is their favorite target—and slowly turn a community's worship toward the Gossamer King. Backwater communities such as Ravenmoor, for example, can find themselves firmly in Ghlaunder's grip in a mere generation or two. Outsiders who investigate too closely might discover that what appear to be distorted rites and outdated local variations of Desnan rituals are actually offerings to the wrong god, with only a select few villagers aware that Ghlaunder is literally siphoning the villagers' worship away from the Tender of Dreams.

Regardless of whether they are open or concealed, rites to Ghlaunder typically take place around stagnant pools or mires, and include chanted invocations, bloodletting rituals, and baptism in foul, larvae-infested waters, all accompanied by the drone of primitive bagpipes, bowed instruments, or hurdy-gurdies. Rituals culminate in living sacrifices suspended above the foul-smelling slough as swarms of mosquitos, stirges, leeches, or worse slowly drain the blood and vitality from the offering. Sacrifices to Ghlaunder are not typically killed by the time the ceremony has concluded. Rather, they are often given a subtle opportunity to escape the unholy ritual, unaware they are actually being purposefully released and ignorant of the virulent diseases they now harbor and will bring back to their kin and community in the coming days and weeks. Ghlaunder's faithful consider the resulting deaths from these efforts the true sacrifices to the Gossamer King.

TEMPLES AND SHRINES

Ghlaunder's faith is inherently disorganized, and large temples and centers of worship are rare in civilized areas. Instead, members tend to congregate near stagnant, mosquito-infested mires, cornfield mazes riddled with rot, or the hidden cesspools of underground sewers. The waterlogged ruins of Oagon in the Sodden Lands are thought to host one of Golarion's few true temples to Ghlaunder. Such locations tend to be breeding grounds for some of Ghlaunder's favored servants, such as mindslaver molds and other intelligent diseased creatures. Chosen supplicants often freely become hosts for these parasitic creatures, considering it a true blessing from the Gossamer King.

A PRIEST'S ROLE

Ghlaunder's mortal servants are tasked with spreading disease and parasites throughout the world. For many, proselytizing can be as easy as the shake of a hand after a disgusting sneeze or passing an infected blanket to a shivering vagrant. But Ghlaunder's priesthood makes an art of the dissemination of filth and sickness. Some work like parasites, infiltrating backwater communities under the guise of benevolent clergy to subvert the worship of the local divinity and redirect devotion toward Ghlaunder. In areas where such manipulation would be recognized, his priests instead work to directly sicken the population by spreading illness in whatever way they can, whether that means tainting wells with excrement or loosing diseased vermin into the streets. The resulting dead serving as fitting sacrifices to the Gossamer King.

Many of the Ghlaunder's clergy come from the lowest rungs of society: grave diggers, rat catchers, and sewer workers can all become sympathetic to the cleansing and equalizing effects disease has on communities. These individuals take their service to Ghlaunder extremely seriously, as it offers them a means of taking vengeance against those of higher station who are more fortunate simply as a consequence of birth or occupation. Many breed diseased creatures themselves—rats, ticks, and stirges are favorites—letting their infected prizes loose into the world to spread their filth. Others intentionally harbor parasites, collecting their eggs to pass forth into the food or water of others so that they, too, can propagate Ghlaunder's brood.

But the spread of disease remains the main motivation for Ghlaunder's clergy, and his priests hatch elaborate schemes to infect entire communities with contagious and deadly diseases. When they can sow discord among other congregations and shift blame toward good-aligned clergy, all the better, as Ghlaunder's clerics seek neither credit nor infamy, taking pride instead for a job well done when the corpses of the dead pile high outside city walls.

Ghlaunder's faith has no centralized organization, with lone wolf clerics and cults often operating independently across Golarion. In many cases, Ghlaunder's priests do not serve as shepherds of their flock, but rather as deceitful peddlers of appropriated faiths and corruptors of a community by whatever means possible. In veneration of Ghlaunder's devious nature, priests prefer slower, subtler methods of infection, and may even live as upright citizens of a community while focusing their efforts on spreading disease to passing travelers (whose deaths then also act as sacrifices to the mosquito god). In those places where the worship of Ghlaunder is less concealed, particularly among humanoid tribes, the god's clerics initiate elaborate rituals to infect all followers with disfiguring diseases. Survivors see themselves as Ghlaunder's blessed,

and they bear the lingering symptoms and resulting scars with pride.

Clerics, druids, and rangers of Ghlaunder, upon first gaining the ability to cast divine spells, can choose to affect vermin instead of animals when using animal-oriented spells (such as *animal shapes*, *detect animals or plants*, and *hide from animals*); these spells can no longer be used to affect animals. Clerics and rangers of Ghlaunder can prepare *summon swarm* as a 2nd-level spell.

ADVENTURERS

Ghlaunder's mortal heralds are tasked with spreading filth wherever they travel, and his acolytes often infiltrate powerful adventuring groups, impersonating evangelists of other faiths to conceal their true motivations. These worshipers take an intense interest in the sickness and rot that dwells in the forgotten places of the world, collecting samples or infecting themselves with dulled-down versions of rare and virulent strains in order to bring them back to civilization for cultivation and dissemination. As with other symbiotic parasites, many adventuring groups do not realize their complicity in

such a process, and by the time the first violent cough or runny nose manifests among their party, it is far too late.

Ghlaunder's supplicants similarly seek to leave illness in their wakes. Worshipers view sickness as a necessary force in the natural world, culling the weak and cleansing the world of the unworthy. They admire the survivability and adaptability of parasites, and emulate these qualities in adventuring parties, manipulating others in order to take more than their fair share of healing and treasure, growing more powerful at the expense of their comrades. Others take this admiration more literally, and offer up their bodies to the foulest symbiotes, sacrificing their themselves—and their sanity—in service to Ghlaunder.

CLOTHING

Ritual garments of Ghlaunder vary widely from region to region, but many cult traditions dictate that ceremonial robes remain undyed and unwashed, resulting in filthy gray attire displaying characteristic red smears from the bloodletting of sacrificial victims. Mosquito-shaped masks are popular accoutrements, though the quality of these masks can range from the twig-and-gourd constructs of rural worshipers to more elaborate jeweled affairs common in urban congregations. Still others don the hollowed and preserved heads of giant mosquitos, and learn to use the barbed proboscises to spill the blood of their enemies.

HOLY TEXT

Though Ghlaunder has no central text of tenets, his clergy are fond of creating what serves as an essential guidebook in the promulgation of sickness. Most examples of these texts are pairings of two separate works hastily rebound as a single tome: *Calgaro's Compendium Pathologica*. This disturbingly illustrated tome of magical and mundane diseases includes the scholar Vesubius' expansive chapter on parasites and symbiotic vermin found in early copies of his seminal work, *Profundus Bestiarum*. Copies of these works in the possession of Ghlaunder's clergy often feature extensive marginalia further outlining the reproductive cycles and habitats of Golarion's deadliest parasites.

HOLIDAYS

Ghlaunder's followers don't observe regular holidays, but instead congregate in the wake of significant meteorological events—especially humid days after heavy rains and floods—when stagnation, mold, and pests multiply most fruitfully. Nights of heavy pollution, when atmospheric distortions seem to enlarge the full moon on the horizon and give it a blood-red cast, are revered spectacles for Ghlaunder's faithful that signal the start of sacred bloodletting ceremonies. The onset of sickness that accompanies the settling winter winds during Lamashan makes this month especially relevant to Ghlaunder's faithful, who seek out the afflicted for sacrifice.

APHORISMS

Common sayings are inconsistent among Ghlaunder's decentralized clergy, but many regional variations exist on the following themes.

Harbor Within, Spread Without: This tenet reflects the modus operandi of many of Ghlaunder's devout clergy; they nurture diseases and parasites in themselves to spread the contagion to others.

In Dreams We Flourish, but Only Sacrifice Feeds the Family: This saying is popular in Ravenmoor, where most are ignorant of the fact their venerations are to Ghlaunder, not Desna. These citizens rely on the false promise of their faith to justify all manner of horrific practices, believing they are only keeping their community safe.

RELATIONS WITH OTHER RELIGIONS

The antagonism between Ghlaunder and Desna extends to their respective churches, with the Gossamer King's cultists infiltrating the Great Dreamer's congregations in attempts to lure them into venerating Ghlaunder. But Desna does not suffer such trespasses alone. Nearly all of Golarion's deities are targets for Ghlaunder's parasitic ways. The cramped quarters used by some parishioners make them vulnerable to the spread of virulent disease. Ghlaunder's worshipers take great delight in watching a flock turn on its clergy when they are suddenly too overtaxed to heal everyone, particularly if it results in the poor becoming violent toward the rich when the latter can afford special curative spells. Alignment matters little to Ghlaunder's clergy in such cases, and Asmodeus's diabolical temples are as tempting of targets as well-to-do churches of Abadar.

Only Lamashtu's devoted seem exempt from such intrusions, with speculation that this is by some secret pact or ancient partnership. Whether Ghlaunder's considerations are out of respect, fear, or reverence is unknown, though some wonder if Ghlaunder has plans to usurp the Mother of Monsters' divine mantle.

Ghlaunder has an intense rivalry with Cyth-V'sug, demon lord of fungus and parasites, as the two are in competition for followers. But other demon lords welcome the Gossamer King as one of their own, and some scholars speculate that Ghlaunder might even be a consort to Gogunta or Mazmezz.

REALM

Ghlaunder makes his home in a swampy quagmire of the Abyss called Bzuulzeel. There, among brackish backwaters, the god's great bulk buzzes in insatiable hunger, hunting the multitude of demons lurking within his marshy realm. The most numerous of these creatures are disgusting omox and hezrou demons evolved from the souls of poisoned and polluted mortals. It is a grand irony that the ultimate fate of devout followers of Ghlaunder who died by such means might be their consumption by their own foul, insatiable god.

PLANAR ALLIES

Ghlaunder attracts all manner of vile creatures to his service, and some may serve the calls of the faithful. The following creatures can be summoned using spells such as *planar ally*.

Bloodbloat (herald of Ghlaunder): This unique blightspawn (*Pathfinder RPG Bestiary 5* 43) takes the same disgusting form as its master—that of a giant, bloated mosquito-thing so large it blocks out the moon. This massive vermin stalks the Great Beyond, seeking to feast on divine blood. The wily creature has successfully drawn the blood of dozens of divine entities, and its hunt extends even to the Material Plane, where it seeks out the mortal spawn of deities and demigods in its endless quest to gorge itself on holy and unholy vitae. It hopes that some mythic virus capable of killing even gods will germinate within its bowels. This creature heeds the call of only Ghlaunder's most devout worshipers, though serving them or consuming them are both equal possibilities for the unpredictable blightspawn.

The Buzzing Mire (unique elder water elemental): Taking the form of a hulking wave of putrid-smelling marsh water, this creature hums with the incessant drone of a million thirsty mosquitos. Usually heaving forth from stagnant sloughs to claim sacrifices given to Ghlaunder, it brings disease in its wake, and its merest touch carries a virulent filth fever. Furthermore, at least two mosquito swarms constantly surround the Buzzing Mire, and squirming larvae continuously hatch from the egg-infested water that makes up the mighty creature's form. The brutish elemental has little consideration of anything but lumbering forth into the mortal world when called, its monotonous murmurs heralding waste and destruction.

Sasserak (unique Gargantuan fiendish dire rat): This enormous demonic rat is a fitting servitor of Ghlaunder. Shiftless and lazy, she is most often found lounging on her back haunches with the bulk of her gigantic, rotting corpulence undulating in doughy waves around her, attended by thousands of her smaller, preening kin. When forced to move, Sasserak drags her dead weight beneath her, and her boil-covered skin tears open to allow swarms of flies, maggots, and litters of diseased, mutated ratlike vermin to spill forth from her sick form. Pestilence follows in her wake; it is no secret that Sasserak desires Ghlaunder's divine mantle, and seeks some foul disease to lay low the Gossamer King himself.

Groetus

Groetus is an apocalyptic god of unknown origins, perhaps predating the current incarnation of the planes. Enigmatic and malevolent, he remains infinitely patient in the face of an indefinite vigil to fulfill his mysterious purpose. Because he does not actively cultivate worshipers, much of what is known about him and his faith is limited and contradictory, built from secondhand lore repeated by scattered—and mostly insane—followers. Most folk pay him no heed or give him only scant consideration, for tangible and immediate threats are far more pressing than a god of the death of all things. This doesn't bother Groetus, for he knows the end times will come, whether mortals believe in him or not.

GOD OF THE END TIMES

God of empty places, oblivion, and ruins

Alignment CN

Domains Chaos, Darkness, Destruction, Madness, Void

Subdomains Catastrophe, Entropy, Insanity, Loss, Night, Stars

Favored Weapon heavy flail

Centers of Worship Geb, Nidal, Sodden Lands, Ustalav

Nationality none

Obedience Preach of the coming end times to a listener who has not yet accepted this truth. If the person leaves or otherwise refuses to listen to you for the full hour, you must find another person to preach to so that you are proselytizing the entire time. Alternatively, if no one at all is available to listen, spend an hour contemplating ways and times the world might end—do so in an empty place where nothing lives and no person except Groetan worshipers have been for at least a month. While you contemplate, deface any surface available to you with unholy images and symbols, such as a skull-like moon. You then gain a +1 sacred or profane bonus on Will saving throws. The type of bonus depends on your alignment— if you're neither good nor evil, you must choose either sacred or profane the first time you perform your obedience, and this choice can't be changed.

> All things fall into ruin. Once the world has passed, He will perhaps grant us, his children, new life. Perhaps we shall be gods. Perhaps, perhaps, perhaps...
>
> —Fragment from a madman's journal

EVANGELIST BOONS

1: Doomsayer (Sp) *doom* 3/day, *augury* 2/day, or *bestow curse* 1/day

2: Consume Essence (Su) As Groetus will one day consume all existence, so do you seek to consume other mortals. Once per day, you can consume the essence of a dead creature. You must touch the target corpse, which can attempt a Fortitude saving throw (DC = 10 + 1/2 your Hit Dice + your Charisma modifier). If it fails this saving throw, the target is destroyed as per *disintegrate*, and you gain 1d8 temporary hit points. These temporary hit points last for a number of hours equal to your Hit Dice.

3: Whispers of Insanity (Su) Once per day as a standard action, you can whisper an insight gleaned from Groetus to shatter the mind of another creature within 30 feet. The target must attempt a Will saving throw (DC = 10 + 1/2 your Hit Dice + your Charisma modifier). If it fails, the target is driven mad by thoughts and concepts far beyond what the brain can handle, as if the workings of Thassilonian magic were revealed to a common ant; it is affected as if by the *insanity* spell. In addition to the normal ways to remove this spell, this ability's

maddening thoughts can be removed using *modify memory*. A successful Knowledge (religion) check (DC = 10 + 1/2 your Hit Dice + your Charisma modifier) reveals this additional way to negate the effect.

EXALTED BOONS

1: Maddening Voice (Sp) *lesser confusion* 3/day, *mad hallucination*^UM 2/day, or *confusion* 1/day

2: Silent Witness (Su) Emulating Groetus, you can observe your surroundings and the people within them without being heeded or harmed. Once per day as a full-round action, you can protect yourself with the effects of *invisibility*, *nondetection*, and *sanctuary* for 10 minutes per Hit Die you possess. Anyone who succeeds at a Will saving throw (DC = 10 + 1/2 your Hit Dice + your Wisdom modifier) or a caster level check (DC = 11 + your Hit Dice) against these effects sees a glimpse of something unfathomable and becomes confused for 1 round unless it succeeds at a second Will save with the same DC.

3: Infinite Patience (Su) You will serve Groetus until the end of the world, no matter how long you must wait. You cannot die of old age, even by magical means, although aging otherwise affects you normally. In addition, once per day as a standard action, you can choose any one action you could ready and define a condition under which you will take that action. Within the next 24 hours, whenever you observe that condition, you can take the chosen action as an immediate action.

SENTINEL BOONS

1: Endbringer (Sp) *true strike* 3/day, *death knell* 2/day, or *keen edge* 1/day

2: Visions of the End (Su) Once per day as a full-round action, you can gain a sudden vision of a target's doom. You gain the benefits of *augury*, *know the enemy*^UM, and *locate weakness*^UC simultaneously, all regarding the same creature or object (even if the spell normally doesn't function with objects) and its death or undoing. You can use the *locate weakness* effect on only the target creature.

3: Frightful Presence (Su) You have looked into oblivion, and its horrors are reflected in your eyes. You can terrify foes as a free action whenever you take an offensive action, such as attacking. Foes within 30 feet of you and with fewer Hit Dice than you must succeed at a Will saving throw or become shaken for a number of rounds equal to your Hit Dice (DC = 10 + 1/2 your Hit Dice + your Charisma modifier). If the victim has 4 or fewer Hit Dice, it becomes panicked instead. Foes with more Hit Dice than you are immune to this ability.

GROETUS AND MADNESS

It is for Groetus alone to know of the end times and their causes, and he has the unique capacity to comprehend them. He has followers only as a side effect of those individuals' mistaken attempts to grasp the forbidden or unknowable (including failed attempts to use *contact other plane* spells). Some sages believe he may not even know he has worshipers.

Most of Groetus's priests bear some kind of insanity. They can still function in society, but their broken minds hear whispers of the god's will, and they hold beliefs that no sane being would embrace. Pages 250–251 of the *Pathfinder RPG GameMastery Guide* have rules for insanities such as amnesia, mania, and paranoia. Note that Groetus's priests are insane even though none of their mental ability scores have been reduced to 0. Also, followers of the god do not see this insanity as an affliction; rather, they see this connection to Groetus as a gift worth celebrating. A priest's insanity can be cured, but unless she immediately rejects Groetus as a patron deity, she relapses in a matter of hours or days.

UNDERSTANDING GROETUS

There are records that Groetus was worshiped in Azlanti and Thassilonian times, though he has no known kinship to Golarion's other gods and there is no evidence he was once a mortal or nature spirit. The proteans and qlippoth have no tales of his appearance or of a time before he existed.

Groetus presides over the end times—the demise of the world, or perhaps the destruction of the multiverse itself. Having silently witnessed billions of souls from countless worlds filter through the Boneyard, he is unconcerned with the fates of individual heroes, villages, or even civilizations. Despite his chaotic alignment, he is an agent of inevitable fate, ensuring that all things pass. He chose this role for himself, the dispassionate observer in balance against the dispassionate judge.

Groetus's role is to close the book on this reality when the final page of its story is told. He knows only how the story ends, and uses that knowledge to piece together what is yet to come—a conflict occurs, this entity survives until the end of the story, this other entity does not, and so on—and what to do next once the tale is finished. His attention is on the final goal and the cosmic dynamics that may enable or delay that goal: the subtle movement of planes against each other, the brooding thoughts of rising gods, and the births and deaths of stars in the remote expanse of space.

Groetus rarely appears in human form, but a few records from ancient Azlant describe him as a tall, slender man wearing a gray, cowled robe that hangs heavily to the floor. He is slightly bent at the neck, as if bearing a great weight on his head, with ashen skin, hollow eyes, and long, smooth hands. His voice is the dry whisper of old paper, his laughter low and breathy, and his inflection archaic or foreign. His feet are bare and covered in soot, as if he had walked through an extinguished fire.

Groetus almost never intervenes directly in the mortal world, as if doing so were against some self-defined code. His rare intervention on behalf of his prophets grants them a few moments of clarity at those critical times when madness would interfere with his intentions. When he is displeased, madness intensifies, phobias are born or triggered, and eyes become cloudy or weep itchy gray fluid.

THE CHURCH

Just as there are dozens of world-ending prophecies and the exact definition of "the end of all things" varies among religions and races, there are many interpretations of Groetus's role. Most of his cultists follow one of these ideologies (called "dooms"), and each doom can be considered a splinter cult of the god's vague faith. Cultists' identification with particular dooms is generally a reflection of the cultists' particular forms of madness and the visions these insanities inspire. Two worshipers with different ideologies may ally with or ignore each other, but rarely do they fight, for time will prove one or both of them wrong. The best-known dooms of Groetus are as follows.

Mouth of Apocalypse: According to this doom, when the end times come, Groetus will consume the shattered pieces of the planes, all the judged souls, and the remnants of every once-living creature, until he is the last thing in the multiverse, floating alone in an endless dark void. Stories differ as to whether the god will literally consume all with his mouth, or whether he will indirectly devour everything through unspecified servants that he will then absorb, or even if all physical and spiritual matter will fly through the void to embed itself within his core. Fanatics of this doom are called the Teeth of Oblivion, and live recklessly, as they expect the world to end at any moment.

Portal of Incarnation: This doom holds that as the last soul is judged and creation erodes, Groetus will collect the greatest essences of heroes, villains, dragons, earth, fire, and other fundamental concepts. While the multiverse collapses and is reformed into something greater than its current state, he will shelter these essences from destruction and distill them into purer forms so they can become the first gods and the raw materials for the next reality. He will then wait countless ages for the cycle to end again. The members of this cult are the Heralds of the Incarnate Moon, and they believe the current world is an impure predecessor to the next, clarified reality. They wish to hasten the cycle so the next world comes sooner, and believe that their souls will be part of the next cycle's gods.

Sign of the Destroyer: Followers of this doom claim Groetus is merely a sign that the end times are nigh, not actually an agent of destruction. He is part of the natural order. Just as ants, humans, and even gods are born and die, so too must all of creation. When his moon approaches the Boneyard and turns red, Golarion's own moon will bear the shadow of a skull to let all mortals know that the end of the world is but days away. Members of this cult call themselves the Followers of the Gray Sign, and they are the most benign members of Groetus's doomsday cult. They are mostly content to preach warnings and observe omens rather than trying to accelerate the end of the world, but they are still prone to unexpected mercy killings and other creepy behavior. They don't know whether the end will be gentle or violent, sudden or drawn out, but like the death of any mortal, it is inevitable.

TEMPLES AND SHRINES

Members of the cult of Groetus have little interest in devoting time to building; they usually take over abandoned or ruined temples of other faiths, or remnants of buildings that were once popular and celebrated places. The most valued sites have windows or holes in the ceiling that allow a view of the full moon. The oldest temples—those that have been used by the cult for thousands of years—tend to conceal strange portals called *Doomsday Doors*. These secret doors are said to open to horrific realms. When the end of the world is nigh, all of these doors will open and unleash various apocalypses upon the world. Loot-crazed adventurers have managed to temporarily open some of these portals; few have defeated the horrors that crawled out, even fewer have investigated what lies beyond the doors, and none have ever returned sane or whole.

For a small cult run by lunatics, the church has a remarkable number of tiny shrines. Most are large rocks aligned toward lunar conjunctions, and carved with symbols of skulls. Strange whispers hiss from the rocks on some nights, especially when they are annointed with the blood of heroes or the essence of destroyed magic.

A PRIEST'S ROLE

Perhaps because Groetus does not intend to create followers or prophets, he has no organized faith. Most of his worshipers are loners—either insane doomsayers who live on the street or more dangerous megalomaniacs who actively seek to bring about the end of existence and please Groetus. They may act alone or attract like-minded followers, depending on the roots of their faith and particular forms of insanity. They are left to their own devices, and their individual activities and duties depend on which doom each believes is paramount.

Groetus's indifference means the mad fools who worship him may do terrible things in his name, but the God of the End Times doesn't care. They may instead do generous, noble, or merciful things in his name, and still he pays no heed. Groetus's clerics are given divine power with almost no responsibility (though they pay for this power with madness). His followers may be insane, desperate, depressed, or lazy sadists who enjoy the suffering of others but don't seek gratification by inflicting pain. The mad ones are broken people who have seen glimpsed a powerful, incomprehensible truth and now spend the rest of their lives trying to understand, remember, or forget it. The desperate and depressed ones believe the current world is a place of misery and pain, and embrace the idea that it will expire soon—whether or not they believe there will be a reward or a new beginning after that end. Those who enjoy the suffering of others believe their victims deserve punishment as part of Groetus's plan, or feel better about their own fate after witnessing harm to another. Many people who deliberately choose to

venerate Groetus enjoy the idea of living without long-term consequences; these folk exist in the moment, not caring how their actions affect others or that they risk being punished for their slights and crimes. If, as the prophets say, the world is to end soon, there is no point in following laws or customs that promote stability in ownership or culture. Groetus's cultists are prone to suicide, either as an attempt to join their god before the end times or to gain some measure of relief from their madness or misery.

Priests of the Mouth of Apocalypse doom encourage others to live as if armageddon were only days away. They steal, murder, and pillage as they see fit, and may ally with other doomsday cults to celebrate the arrival of the end of everything. Priests of the Portal of Incarnation doom scrutinize everyone they meet, mentally cataloguing those whose essences are worthwhile and dismissing those who have no value (though this perception is filtered by madness and may have no basis in reality). They may sacrifice the "worthy" ones to speed their souls to the afterlife and Groetus's collection. Priests of the Sign of the Destroyer doom speak prophesies in public, warn others about horrible fates, and generally make nuisances of themselves in peaceful societies. Regardless of their dooms, Groetus's priests have a morbid curiosity about the dead and dying, and frequently use *deathwatch* to observe others. They are unpopular among adventurers because they often refuse to heal even the most gravely injured allies, believing that healing only staves off the inevitable deaths dealt by monsters.

Groetus's clerics can prepare *fear* as a 4th-level spell, and those with the Madness or Void domain can prepare *lesser confusion* as a 2nd-level spell and *confusion* as a 4th-level spell.

ADVENTURERS

Followers of Groetus who aren't prone to mad ravings or grand plans tend to be skulkers and hangers-on, content to lurk near battlefields or in the rear of adventuring parties, watching the conflict unfold and taking action only at the end of a fight, and then just to dispatch the wounded—an act of mercy that sickly parallels the morbid interests of their god. The desperate and depressed do this out of compassion, and feel jealous for the dead; the casually sadistic do it because it lets them feel important, as tools of the god's will; the mad do it because the voices or visions suggest it must be done.

CLOTHING

Formal raiment for the church is a light gray robe with pale blue trim. The exact shade varies from region to region and prophet to prophet, but is always some form of gray with blue accents. Most priests put little stock

in their appearance (after all, they are anticipating the end of all things), and their clothing tends to become shabby and stained as the years go by. Many allow their hair to grow long and unkempt, but some shave their heads and dab dark blue paint or makeup around their eyes to represent the dreaded skull-moon image of their strange god.

Holy Text As most of his clergy are insane, there is no codified list of Groetus's teachings, only fragments collected from the journals of the mad, scrawled ramblings written on asylum walls and the skins of murder victims. Much of it is unclear or contradictory.

Book of the Last Moon: The more rational members of the church keep this compilation of scraps of lore; most readers find it disturbing and have nightmares after reading it.

HOLIDAYS

Despite their rampant madness and tendency to group in independent cells, the faithful of Groetus are united in celebrating one holiday.

The Final Day: On the last day of the year, the faithful pray silently for an hour at sundown, hoping for guidance from Groetus or a sign that the end times will come soon. Some cults follow this with other rituals such as sacrifices and chanting.

APHORISMS

Groetus's mad prophets often utter these phrases.

The Patient Moon Pulls the Tides: The moon creates the high and low tides that wear away the shores and strand sea creatures on the beach. Even the mightiest cliffs eventually collapse into the water. Haste and urgency may not be the best course.

Ruin for Everything: Every single living thing—even the world and the planes—is doomed, and will be torn apart at the end of everything. Do not grow attached to friends, wealth, or even the familiar configurations of mountains and rivers, for one day they will be gone, and that foolish sentimentality will have been wasted.

RELATIONS WITH OTHER RELIGIONS

Groetus has little to do with any other divinities. Because of the maddening influence of his skull-moon, the other gods and goddesses are very cautious about how they approach Groetus in the infrequent times they need to communicate with him. Even Pharasma does not contact him more than she absolutely must. It is known that the souls in Pharasma's Court draw his moon-realm closer, and a few are aware that the crystallized souls of true atheists repel him—both incidentally by their proximity, and sometimes directly when the Lady of Graves "feeds" him the essence of one (though whether this is a literal feeding or a transfer of essence is unknown) to push him away. It is believed that a planar apocalypse will occur when his moon contacts the Spire itself, and even violent gods (save Rovagug) agree this is something that should be forestalled as long as possible. However, in the short term, most gods seem to simply ignore Groetus, and their priests rarely seek out his cults.

Mouth of the Apocalypse cultists often ally with the cult of Urgathoa because of their common interest in indulgence, though the nihilists scoff at the idea of living forever as undead. Rovagug is another rumored ally of Groetus because of their common interest in destruction; the followers of both gods avoid interfering with each others' plans, though neither has been observed directly aiding the other.

REALM

The skull-moon of Groetus looms above Pharasma's Boneyard. The appearance of Groetus's moon varies slightly from viewer to viewer, and as there is no accurate way to judge celestial distances in the planar realms (where the thoughts of gods or the weight of a million souls can bend space), it is impossible to determine any correlation between the moon and mortal disasters. At its smallest known size, it looks no larger than a thumbnail held at arm's length; at its largest, it appears to be 20 times that size.

Because the ravings of his priests contradict each other, mortals are unsure whether this moon is actually the god, his realm, a shell containing him, or something he protects. In truth, it is all these things. It is Groetus in physical form, like an impossibly huge avatar. It is his realm, much as an ancient tree is both a living thing and a home to smaller creatures (his servants and petitioners). It is a shell, physically separating the multiverse from its end.

These overlapping truths are too much for lesser minds to experience and survive intact. Some who dare set foot upon the moon vanish instantly; others walk there for a time and return on their own with twisted minds, speaking fragments of prophecy about the end times. Those who have attempted to scry its surface see strange writing that writhes and folds upon itself, leading the viewers' eyes and thoughts along intricate paths until it eventually drives the scryers mad, turns them into prophets of Groetus,

or both. This outcome occurs whether the traveler or diviner is mortal, undead, an outsider, or a servant of another god.

PLANAR ALLIES

Groetus makes no effort to create unique servants, but many creatures have fallen under his power by traveling to his moon-realm. The following are well-known supernatural servitors of Groetus, suitable for conjuring with *planar ally* or similar spells.

End's Voice (herald of Groetus): End's Voice (*Pathfinder Adventure Path #64: Beyond the Doomsday Door* 84) is an enigmatic creature that is both more and less mysterious than its master. It looks like a giant shrouded figure floating above the ground, legless, faceless, and wielding a heavy flail with ends made of glowing energy. Although often confused with a reaping undead, it is a living outsider and seems mildly insulted when others assume otherwise. Its voice is hollow and distorted, colored with accents from ruined empires and dead languages. It comes to Golarion only rarely, usually as a silent witness to a great slaughter upon the battlefield or the last gasp of a dying city, though it may strike out at seemingly random wounded or dying targets, as if making sure they die as expected. When called by mortals, the herald demands specific deeds of death, injury, or destruction that further the end of times. It might ask that every third adult male in a village be branded on the face with a mysterious symbol, or that a prince with black hair be nearly drowned, or a castle's eastern wall be cracked but left standing. Usually, these acts have no apparent link to the conjurer's needs, and most create a series of events that takes years or decades to play out. It favors the burning of incense and exotic woods, lingering over the fragrant smoke and contorting itself strangely.

Geg Noam Gyeg (barbed devil): Geg Noam Gyeg is paranoid and adorns its spikes with the eyes of its victims so it can watch in all directions. It prefers payment in silver mirrors and divination-based magic items.

Yles (naunet protean): This gray naunet (*Pathfinder RPG Bestiary 2* 216) is more insane than others of its kind, and constantly babbles narration of its current activities. It collects spellbooks and other magical writings.

INTRODUCTION

ACHAEKEK

ALSETA

APSU

BESMARA

BRIGH

DAHAK

GHLAUNDER

GROETUS

GYRONNA

HANSPUR

KURGESS

MILANI

NADERI

SIVANAH

ZYPHUS

Gyronna

The goddess Gyronna plays shepherd to wayward hate and coddles the entitlement and darkness in mortal hearts. The superstitious and crass describe Gyronna as both the Angry Hag and the Hag Queen, goddess of scorned women. While her priesthood does consist largely of women used and cast aside by society, she represents a much darker impulse than mere wounded pride. Gyronna is the briar that springs from bitter soil; her purview is not scorn, but the hatred that festers around a wounded heart never allowed to heal and the dread things that grow from small and thoughtless evils. When trust and love fail, her embrace fills that void with the strength of seething vengeance and bitter entitlement.

THE ANGRY HAG

Goddess of extortion, hatred, and spite

Alignment CE

Domains Chaos, Destruction, Evil, Madness

Subdomains Demon, Insanity, Nightmare, Rage

Favored Weapon dagger

Centers of Worship Lake Encarthan region, River Kingdoms

Nationality Kellid

Obedience Spend at least 30 minutes working to make another sentient creature's life measurably worse or more miserable, whether by destroying its property, sabotaging its efforts, or afflicting it magically. Your victim must survive this encounter, but your actions can indirectly lead to its death, such as tainting a plague-ridden man's medicine or stealing the money a woman would use to pay back a loan. You must make your victim aware of your involvement, and always name some price or task your victim can perform to assuage your bitter heart and gain recompense for the damage you have inflicted, though this price does not need to be reasonable. You gain a +4 profane bonus on Intimidate checks.

EVANGELIST BOONS

1: Dread Gifts (Sp) *fumbletongue*[UM] 3/day, *disfiguring touch*[UM] 2/day, or *eruptive pustules*[UM] 1/day

2: Rot Their Minds (Su) Your spewed curses and venomous retorts take on a malevolent timbre, and your enemies' minds bend before the potency of your ire. Once per day, you can cast *feeblemind*, as per the spell, except *remove curse* can remove this effect, as can *heal*, *limited wish*, *miracle*, and *wish*. If the target fails its Will saving throw against this effect, it recognizes you as its afflictor. After this effect ends, if you are within 30 feet of the target, it is shaken for a number of rounds equal to your Hit Dice or until you move more than 30 feet away from it (whichever comes first). This is a curse effect.

3: Mother of Curses (Su) The rage within your heart shields you against harm and turns it back on others. You gain an amount of spell resistance equal to 11 + your Hit Dice, but only against necromancy and transmutation spells, as well as enchantment spells of the charm subschool. Once per day, when a spell fails to penetrate your spell resistance, you can reflect it back on its caster, as if using *spell turning*.

EXALTED BOONS

1: Alone Among Many (Sp) *youthful appearance*[UM] 3/day, *undetectable alignment* 2/day, or *nondetection* 1/day

"Depraved," they bellow at that which they covet. "Unforgiveable," they label her crimes, which they once gleefully committed upon her without shame. Ours are not the words of hypocrites. Ours is hate worn without a coward's mask.

—*Black Ledger of Macy Swain*

2: Come by Night (Ex) Night is when others are vulnerable and trusting, and few can pierce the darkness to see your handiwork. You gain darkvision 30 feet and are immune to any magical *sleep* effects (this functions identically to an elf's immunity to magical *sleep* effects).

3: Curdled Trust (Su) You can sow the seeds of distrust in a group and assign the blame for your actions to another. Once per day, upon committing an evil act or casting a spell in front of witnesses, as a free action you can enchant all onlookers to believe another person known to them committed that act. If you know a creature's full name, you can name it specifically as the culprit. Otherwise, each onlooker sees a random friend or family member committing your actions. Onlookers who succeed at a Will saving throw (DC = 10 + 1/2 your Hit Dice + your Wisdom modifier) are not fooled, though they might still be fooled by concealing clothing or mundane disguises you may be wearing. This is a mind-affecting enchantment effect.

SENTINEL BOONS

1: Malice (Sp) *ray of sickening*[UM] 3/day, *blindness/deafness* 2/day, or *excruciating deformation*[UM] 1/day

2: Cloak of Curses (Su) You surround yourself in a shroud of whispered secrets and spiteful swearing, distorting the world around you and repelling others with the bitterness in your heart. Once per day, you can activate your cloak of curses as a standard action, and maintain it for up to 1 minute per Hit Die you possess. While the cloak is active, creatures of the animal and vermin type will not approach within 5 feet of you and move away if you approach them. Attacks from all other creatures suffer a 20% miss chance. This miss chance increases to 30% if the attacking creature is lawful or good (this miss chance does not stack). Creatures that succeed at a Will saving throw (DC = 10 + 1/2 your Hit Dice + your Charisma modifier) are not affected by your cloak of curses.

3: Never Suffer Alone (Ex) Misery is a gift you have received far too much of, and you have learned to reflect it onto others. Three times per day, when an opponent successfully deals hit point damage to you, you can immediately make an attack of opportunity against the creature that damaged you, even if you could not normally make an attack of opportunity. You can attack normally with this attack of opportunity or target the triggering creature with one of the spells granted by the malice boon above (though doing so provokes an attack of opportunity if an opponent is in melee with you). You can use this ability only once per round.

THE HAG QUEEN

Gyronna's priestesses claim—though only when their goddess's eye is turned away—that upon her first ascension to godhood, the Angry Hag found herself unnaturally fecund, and birthed endless daughters. Her first seven she devoured. The next seven she crushed beneath a great stone. And the daughters thereafter she cast down into the dust. The seven she devoured further gestated in their mother's bile, and eventually sprang from her chest as the first night hags, every bit as wicked as their mother. The seven she crushed were found by Pharasma, who nurtured the infant souls as they learned compassion and matured into the first memitim psychopomps.

But the daughters beyond those found themselves adopted by mortal families, and loved as mortal children, and became the first changelings. Gyronna watched these children with disgust, but one by one, the world failed each girl in turn, blackening their hearts through ignorance, loss, or cruelty, and they inevitably found their way back to their true mother. Gyronna rewarded them with the same painful ascension she'd endured, tearing the lingering goodness from their mortal forms and transforming each daughter into a progenitor for her own breed of hag; thus, an untold number of early hags may have become the founders of new hag lines. Even today, changelings remain Gyronna's favored servants, for each is but a moment's cruelty away from crawling pitifully back into her mother's arms.

UNDERSTANDING GYRONNA

Few sources agree on Gyronna's origin, and her cults quietly hunt anyone who investigates it. Many place her origins in the First World, as a malicious fey princess who delighted in manipulation for her own amusement. After crossing a powerful rival—Baba Yaga or Magdh, by most accounts—the immortal dilettante was punished with deformities and cast into the mortal realm. Other stories describe her as a trio of bickering sisters who befell the same fate, and were so mutilated that they were forced to lean on one another to even stand, eventually growing together into one loathsome, hateful whole. In the wake of such exile, kindness and civility are, to her, dribbles of poisoned honey, and Gyronna would burn all the world to ash to eradicate such mockery and deception.

Gyronna's complete figure is rarely depicted; she is more often represented as the same bloodshot eye her followers use as their unholy symbol. Her rare manifestations are chaotic, shifting form mid-conversation—sometimes decrepit, other times vibrantly young, beautiful, withered and dead, jubilant, weeping, or raging. According to ancient tales, the Angry Hag has no true form beyond the singular bulging eye through which she sees the shadows cast by even the brightest lights. Only her gender remains constant—though she presents vastly differing images of womanhood—as do the ragged vestments in which she wraps herself.

The Angry Hag's favor is felt in misfortune befalling those who vex her followers, or in small, suffering animals left in one's home by stray cats. Those who earn her ire can expect minor social blunders to grow far beyond their expected scope, premature aging, or for their touch to wither plants and sicken animals.

THE CHURCH

Order and hierarchy disgust Gyronna, and her faith is one of hidden cults—referred to as circles—spread by hushed whispers and desperate midnight indoctrinations. Her teachings emphasize personal fulfillment and rejection of the hollow trappings of society unless they suit one's needs. Chief among her cultists are women in troubled marriages, who have found themselves either betrayed by the person they trusted most in the world, or punished and exiled from their community for betraying that same trust. The hurt from such encounters, or similar rejections and violations of trust, plants the seed Gyronna's faith cultivates into poisonous fruit. No wound of spite is unjustified and no price of revenge is too high; all past agony demands new suffering from others.

Individual adherents may act openly or in secret, but circles of Gyronnans nearly always meet in seclusion, concealing their identities under hoods or behind masks. Meeting by night in untamed wilderness or in crumbling structures where vermin and rot dominate, her faithful trade secrets, offer prayers and sacrifices, exchange poisons and black magic, and cajole one another into assisting with personal rituals or plots. Leadership is determined by whichever member can cow her sisters into compliance or recruit enough followers to overpower challengers. Hags or cruel changelings often lead a circle, while a full hag coven may command large and influential cults to act as their eyes and ears across a broader area. In such cases, Gyronna's mortal worshipers serve almost entirely as agents for their mistress's whims, helping to enact schemes, secure victims for torture, and kidnap healthy infants to exchange for their own changeling brood.

Gyronna's faith consists almost entirely of women, but is by no means a religion that glorifies or protects her chosen gender. Women outside her faith—and even the unwary within it—are considered apt targets for violence, extortion, and curses. Key among her philosophy is nurturing the entitlement that accompanies a life touched by wealth, beauty, or political power, and her church has little use for the poor or other groups forced to society's margins. While the bitter-hearted among these groups may participate in her cults, they rarely earn the goddess's favor or any measure of influence unless they also wield formidable magical abilities. Her cult has no particular interest in challenging gender-related prejudices or improving the lot of women in general; most would rather use oppressive gender roles or assumptions to conceal their activities or lay a foundation of hatred in potential future converts.

While Gyronna's worship is predominantly practiced by women, this is more because the goddess finds the anger of men to be blunt and clumsy. She is a vintner of malevolence, keen to grow a cold, bitter heart over months or years, and has no use for worshipers who fall prey to the self-aggrandizement or lack of self-awareness she believes men embody. She is known to strike those men who beg her favor with impotence, claiming it calms their temperament. The threat of such a result drives most men away, but a select few find her potential support for their vendettas and resentment to be worth the risk, and eventually find a place within her cult.

TEMPLES AND SHRINES

As Gyronna is a secretive and paranoid goddess, her followers rarely construct elaborate temples. Instead, they claim sites of great natural beauty that are isolated from prying eyes, and dedicate them to the Angry Hag. Each site is christened with an altar of piled stones, capped with a fist-sized stone painted to resemble an eye, or with an enormous gem, among more influential circles. Followers claim that Gyronna—as well as any hags who serve the cult—can see through these stones to cast judgment and dispense curses. Especially ambitious circles have been known to erect elaborate monuments or rings of standing stones upon sites of natural wonder in mockery of the fey or druidic protectors from whom they seized these sites.

Sites frequented by Gyronna's priestesses develop a dimness and dankness that meld into a sense of looming dread. Venomous creatures and plants flourish in and around her shrines. Adherents of the Angry Hag mark these spaces in ways obvious only to the faithful. In urban settings, these demarcations appear as motifs of three concentric circles—resembling an eye—worked into decorations and stonework, while in rural environs a circle may hang woven spheres or circles from tree branches or paint eye imagery onto trees and rocks. Such territorial markings are intended to warn off other Gyronnans, but cultists consider such subtle and contextual messages to be sufficient warnings for all trespassers, and maintain that any who stumble into their territory deserve whatever fate befalls them.

A PRIEST'S ROLE

Most women find their way to Gyronna's arms after a humiliating downfall or painful personal experience, and find new purpose in exposing the same weakness or hypocrisy in others. Worshipers of the Angry Hag believe that nothing and no one can be truly selfless or worthy of redemption, and that all who aspire to goodness have some disgusting truth they hide from the world. A priestess's role is to uncover this hidden truth and pluck and pick at it to make these supposedly moral souls dance to her whims, until they finally admit—broken, ruined, and sobbing—that altruism and all their good deeds were lies told to hide a rotten core. A priestess of Gyronna knows herself to be a monster, but believes she is a monster of circumstance, formed by the malice of the world and willing to admit her terrible truth rather than hiding it from herself.

Gyronna's faith divides roughly into urban and rural sects, though both are highly informal affairs of superstition more than strict adherence. Urban worshipers live a double life, fitting seamlessly into their middle-class or high-society lives by day and working fell magic by night. Rural sects, in contrast, operate largely in the open, trusting fear of their magic and inevitable reprisal to keep the scattered people of the countryside from standing against them. Most operate at night, roaming their territory during dusk and dawn, and Gyronnans in isolated settings brazenly demand alms, food, or lodging from those whose paths they cross during these transitional hours.

As a follower of Gyronna grows in power and experience, her tolerance for others dwindles until she can no longer stomach the presence of

her own sisters. These rare elders retreat from society, hiding deep in the wilderness or sealing themselves within lonely estates, and visit terrible and protracted deaths upon any who violate their homes. They spend their days in meditation or communion with the Outer Planes, hoping to learn some foul new untruth regarding the nature of creation that has thus far gone unexposed, and in so doing, earn a place at their goddess's side as one of the immortal Daughters of Gyronna who tend her infernal realm. Clerics of Gyronna can prepare *eyebite* as a 6th-level spell.

ADVENTURERS

The worshipers of Gyronna are monsters made, rather than born, and few begin their careers in her service. Those who serve her directly do so by undermining forces of compassion and prestige, often out of spite for those same organizations' failures to protect or provide

for them. Recruiting a few dissatisfied housewives or the workers in a miserable brothel may grant a priestess access to many private conversations or let her spread disease or cursed afflictions, all the while undermining the trust between the town's inhabitants.

In the River Kingdoms, Gyronna sees many casual worshipers and momentary invocations. Many beg her favor or donate to her cultists to ward off bad luck. Bitter and abused women along the untamed frontier may invoke her name to curse an ex-lover or punish men who cross them, hoping to draw the Angry Hag's attention upon such targets even if the supplicant doesn't honor her directly. Especially superstitious folks may even retain a Gyronnan priestess in the hope that she will ward away other dark forces that stalk them.

CLOTHING

Gyronnans mark their divine awakening by retaining the same clothing they ritually don when their eyes first opened to the goddess's sacred truths, along with a black smock representing the wrongs done to them and their transition to her faith. These outfits, or "shabbles," quickly turn a filthy gray, and Gyronnans sometimes accentuate the clothes they wear under their smocks with pink splotches, like the veins of their goddess's bloodshot eye. Over time, these vestments and smocks invariably grow ragged and patched, and even the grandest gown transforms into an unsightly rag. Pristine shabbles are the sign of a neophyte worshiper, as distinct and embarrassing as a child's jumper.

HOLY TEXT

Gyronna's faith is spread through hushed whispers and colorful invectives. While no single holy book binds them, many priestesses maintain black ledgers filled with gossip, dreams, blackmail material, and the identities of fellow zealots, as well as lists of enemies and the myriad wrongs they've committed. The ledgers of especially old or powerful priestesses become akin to holy books in their own right.

Black Ledger of Macy Swain: Among the most famous of these holy books, this ledger contains the writings of a Gyronnan witch tried shortly before the death of Aroden and executed via poison, hanging, disemboweling, drowning, beheading, and finally, burial, even as her head still screamed curses at her accusers.

HOLIDAYS

Most circles meet under the new moon—fewer souls can witness what transpires on moonless nights, and superstition claims that midnight on these dark nights is when the Angry Hag blinks her ageless eye, and that looking upon her work when it reopens pleases her.

Blightmother's Eve: The final new moon of each year stands out as a night of toil among Gyronnans, who use the occasion to make sacrifices and work powerful rituals. Their ultimate hope is to rejuvenate the bitter crone, in hopes that she enters the new year with slightly more patience for her wretched mortal followers.

APHORISMS

Priestesses of the Angry Hag especially love blistering invectives and clever insults. Some are purely odious, while others wax poetic, but a bitter heart backs each, and calls to its kin.

Blessed Are the Maids Who Find Nothing so Odious to Endure as Peace: Sometimes shortened to "this odious peace," or "blessed, odious girl," the most common Gyronnan aphorism praises women who stir up trouble and cannot abide quiet and easy days.

Weeds Spring from Waste: Gyronnans are quick to remind each other and outsiders that their wickedness grew from a far more wretched source, and the bleak deeds they enact were often set in motion by those they seek to punish.

RELATIONS WITH OTHER RELIGIONS

Gyronna is most closely associated with her fellow Kellid god, Hanspur, and the clergy of each pay grudging respect to those of the other. Gyronnan priestesses are expected to spare Hanspur's servants from their extortions and violence, and in return, those who worship the Water Rat offer safe passage and shelter along the waterways.

Among the philosophies and portfolios of the more popular gods of the Inner Sea, Gyronna's hew most closely to Lamashtu's; in the River Kingdoms and along the shores of Lake Encarthan, there is occasional overlap between the human worshipers of both goddesses.

Beyond these connections, Gyronna despises other deities and busies herself in plotting their downfalls. To that end, she disrupts the worshipers of other gods and blackmails their servants, as much for her personal empowerment as to expose their hypocrisy and prove that all the world is just as shallow, selfish, and cruel as her own twisted heart. She hates Pharasma, whom she accuses of stealing away those children she murdered so long ago and poisoning them against their mother. She holds similar contempt for the demon lord Mestama, calling the vile woman a pale imitation of herself and a false mother to her children. Some planar scholars whisper that Mestama and Gyronna are actually twin aspects of the same being, though few advocates of this blasphemous theory survive long.

REALM

Gyronna rules the twisted, midnight forest of Muravelara, an Abyssal realm where the sun never rises and the trees themselves seem to press in and overwhelm travelers. Massive toads and feral cats stalk the shadows, alongside hags and female vrocks. The Hag Queen herself is rarely in residence, preferring to wander the Material Plane, while leaving the forest in the care of her daughters—both literal and honorary. The Daughters of Gyronna guide her petitioners in sacrifices and hunts in between long periods of flagellation and abuse, and all manner of trespassers are captured for drawn-out dismemberment, sacrifice, and regeneration, only to finally be burned alive as torches for special ceremonies conducted under the realm's bloodshot moon.

PLANAR ALLIES

Hags of all breeds ultimately answer to Gyronna's cruel whimsy and make up the bulk of her loyal servants. Night hags and fiendish hags are both suitable servitors to answer a Gyronnan priestess's *planar ally* summons. Within this vile legion, a few servants stand out.

Daughters of Gyronna (unique fiendish hags): Those hags and mortal women who commit atrocities of note join the Angry Hag's side in death as rulers of her Abyssal realm. Each hag claims a specific wicked deed as her purview, and coddles petitioners who earned Gyronna's favor by committing it. They're said to always number thirteen thirteens, and any new addition to this host must first slay whichever daughter she intends to replace and feed upon the daughter's festering liver.

Hebdanke (herald of Gyronna): The seven daughters who Gyronna devoured lived on in their mother's hide as wretched boils before bursting forth as the first night hags, and the youngest emerged a twisted and hideous beast, unable to cloak her hideousness in the guise of beauty like her sisters. The horrible honesty of Hebdanke's face earned her an eternal place as Gyronna's twisted right hand, and as perhaps the only thing the Angry Hag genuinely loves. In place of the ability to twist her own flesh into beauty, Hebdanke is instead blessed with a touch that twists others' beauty into repulsiveness, allowing her to reshape unborn children in Gyronna's image.

Nyvuss (unique CE silvanshee): Once the curious and lovable feline familiar of the Kellid witch Marganala, Nyvuss watched as her mistress's disguised green hag lover lured her deeper into corruption. When Taldan authorities finally lashed her to a pyre for her crimes, the witch swore her soul to Gyronna if only the hag goddess would allow her to take the grand prince's head. The Angry Hag obligingly stitched the burned witch and her familiar into one horrible whole, and under the next new moon, Grand Prince Rodivarian III tripped over a black cat and broke his neck in the fall. Ever since, the mad Nyvuss has served as Gyronna's messenger, spy, and courier of foul luck, always darting in shadows and moving by night so none can see the still-twitching human face stitched into her bloated stomach.

Hanspur

Hanspur is most commonly worshiped in the freedom-loving River Kingdoms. While there are few canonical texts associated with his faith, most legends claim he originally worshiped Gozreh during the tumultuous Age of Darkness before ascending to divinity himself. While the exact details surrounding Hanspur's apotheosis vary, common threads within these tales suggest that a traveling companion drowned him in the Sellen River, and that Gozreh raised him from the dead to serve as a protector of rivers and waterways. But while Hanspur watches over the waters, he cares less for the lives of a river's travelers and not at all about their morality.

THE WATER RAT

God of river travel, rivers, and smugglers

Alignment CN

Domains Chaos, Death, Travel, Water

Subdomains Exploration, Murder, Rivers, Trade

Favored Weapon trident

Centers of Worship River Kingdoms

Nationality Kellid

Obedience With the assistance of another priest of Hanspur or by yourself, simulate the act of drowning. You can do this by fully submerging yourself in a body of water, exhaling all of your breath, and painfully inhaling water instead of air. Alternatively, you can lie on your back with your head at a lower elevation than your legs while water is slowly poured on your face and up your nose. If you choose the latter method, you must cover your face with a cloth while the water is poured. When you conclude this simulated drowning, contemplate your life and how your goals coincide with the teachings of Hanspur and the Six River Freedoms. You gain a +4 sacred or profane bonus on Survival checks attempted while on or near rivers. The type of bonus depends on your alignment—if you're neither good nor evil, you must choose either a sacred bonus or a profane bonus the first time you perform your obedience, and this choice can't be changed.

> Life is suffering. How we choose to allay our agony determines who we are. All must make this choice, and in choosing find their true selves.
>
> —Apocryphal annotations of the Six River Freedoms

EVANGELIST BOONS

1: River Sage (Sp) *hydraulic push*APG 3/day, *river whip*ACG 2/day, or *hydraulic torrent*APG 1/day

2: River Scion (Su) Just as drowning was not the end of Hanspur's story, inhaling water holds no terror for you. As a free action you can breathe underwater, as if affected by *water breathing*, for a number of hours per day equal to the number of Hit Dice you possess. These hours need not be used consecutively, but must be used in 1-hour increments.

3: River's Embodiment (Sp) The river is a part of you, and you are a part of it. Once per day as a standard action, you can transform yourself into a Huge water elemental, as per *elemental body IV*. You can stay in this form for 1 minute per Hit Die you possess, and can dismiss this effect as a free action.

EXALTED BOONS

1: River Guide (Sp) *obscuring mist* 3/day, *haunting mists*UM 2/day, or *aqueous orb*APG 1/day

2: River Traveler (Su) A priest of Hanspur should never fear the water, and should move as freely as the fish (and rats) that make their homes within it. As a free action, you can grant yourself and any allies within 30 feet of you a swim speed of 60 feet. This effect lasts for 1 round per Hit Die you possess or until you dismiss it as a free action, whichever comes first. Your allies must remain within 30 feet of you or lose this benefit. In addition, you gain a +2 profane or sacred bonus (of the same type as that provided by your obedience) on saves against spells with the water descriptor.

3: River's Depths (Su) The river is your companion, and it fights on your behalf, teaching your enemies about the holy act of drowning. Once per day as a standard action, you can cause one creature within 30 feet to begin drowning, filling its lungs with water. The target of this ability can attempt a Fortitude save (DC = 10 + 1/2 your Hit Dice + your Wisdom modifier) to negate the effect. If the target succeeds, it is staggered for 1 round while it gasps for breath. On a failed save, the target immediately begins to suffocate. On the target's next turn, it falls unconscious and is reduced to 0 hit points. One round later, the target drops to –1 hit points and is dying. One round after that, the target dies. Each round, the target can attempt a Fortitude save to end the effect. This ability affects only living creatures that must breathe and cannot breathe underwater. This is a curse effect.

SENTINEL BOONS

1: River Warden (Sp) *wave shield*ACG 3/day, *masterwork transformation*UM 2/day, or *quench* 1/day

2: River Champion (Su) The river is your weapon. Three times per day as a standard action, you can sculpt water into the form of a melee weapon with which you are proficient (typically a trident, but it could also take the form of a dagger or another light weapon). You must have enough water to form the weapon, an amount equal to the weapon's normal weight. Once formed, the weapon behaves as a weapon of its type with an enhancement bonus of +1. This bonus increases by 1 for every 5 additional Hit Dice you have beyond 5 (up to a maximum of +4 at 20 Hit Dice). This weapon deals double the normal amount of damage to creatures with the fire subtype. The weapon dissolves into ordinary water after a number of rounds equal to your Hit Dice or as soon as it leaves your hand, whichever happens first.

3: River's Renewal (Su) As Hanspur was reborn in the water, so too are you healed by it. When completely submerged in water, you gain fast healing 2. You can recover a total number of hit points equal to twice your Hit Dice in this manner each day. At 20th level, if you fall below 0 hit points and your body is fully submerged in a river, you automatically stabilize.

UNDERSTANDING HANSPUR

Clerics of Hanspur, who are indoctrinated in the deeper mysteries of his faith, know that their god was not merely murdered by a traveling companion. The companion was a priest of the daemonic harbinger Corosbel, and the murder was a sacrificial ritual intended to consign Hanspur's soul to the Horseman of Death, Charon, with whom Corosbel wished to gain favor. However, the ritual sacrifice did not proceed as planned. Though the details of what went awry are unclear, Hanspur's clerics believe Gozreh subtly interceded, preventing Corosbel from claiming the entirety of Hanspur's soul for Abaddon. The remainder was bound within Hanspur's dire rat companion, Ashkaelae. Hanspur returned from death a week after the attempted sacrifice, rising from the Sellen River as a demigod with his latent mortal soul fractured. This transformation left him callous and cold. It is unclear whether Gozreh intended for Hanspur to emerge from the waters as a divine being or merely as a divine servitor; the inscrutable nature deity's lukewarm support of Hanspur suggests either that she did not intend for the Water Rat to ascend or that she is not entirely pleased with Hanspur's subsequent actions and attitudes.

Hanspur's mortal identity is a matter of contention among his priests, with different sects of his faithful claiming he was born to their people. Most notably, among Hanspur's Kellid followers, he is depicted as a legendary and ancient Kellid king whose death and attempted sacrifice signaled the fall of the Kellid people and the coming encroachment of southerners. Such followers of Hanspur believe that he ruled the region of the world now known as the River Kingdoms, and that by conquering the rivers in his name, they can reclaim their lost lands for themselves.

Whatever his true origin, Hanspur and his faithful haunt the Sellen River as vengeful guardians, hunting down followers of Corosbel and protecting river travelers from hazards of the waterways.

THE CHURCH

Hanspur's faith is largely decentralized, with no formal hierarchy and considerable variation in the traditions and tenets of the faith between different congregations. Services and prayers draw more from local traditions and the ethics of communities supported by the waterways than from any set religious doctrine. Worship often takes place along the banks of rivers or aboard ferries and boats actively traveling over water. Hanspur's priests rarely conduct formal services, though some faithful take the opportunity to proselytize while ferrying a captive audience downriver.

Typical worshipers of Hanspur include ferry operators, fishers, river pirates, and smugglers. Hanspur's faithful maintain boats, ply the river, and offer passage for a price. More often than not, they live off the land and water, and one of the few teachings common to most of the Water Rat's congregations is instruction in how to recognize and use the gifts of the river. Hanspur thus tends to inspire worship from the destitute and homeless living in the River Kingdoms, offering them both a purpose in life and a path to self-sufficiency.

Hanspur's followers often eschew rites practiced by more organized religions, such as marriage or funerals. Death is a fact of life, and bodies are burned on floating barges with little ceremony, more to protect others from disease and the waters from contamination than from any spiritual belief. Among Hanspurites, both parents typically raise children, but as the saying goes, "The river is always moving," and sometimes it is better for one of the parents to move on.

Hanspur's faithful consider rats sacred animals, honoring them in memory of Hanspur's companion Ashkaelae. Worshipers tend to keep rats, either as pets or simply as signs of their god's favor. Despite this status, the faithful have no compunctions about eating rats as sustenance when the need arises, and Hanspur does not punish his faithful for these acts. Ratfolk followers of Hanspur see Ashkaelae as the true divinity and Hanspur as a revenant or servant of Ashkaelae's will. Curiously, these heretic priests are still granted spells.

Hanspur communicates to his priests through images reflected in river water. Because of the incomplete state of Hanspur's soul, his faithful sometimes have a difficult time interpreting the meaning behind these ambiguous visions. Unscrupulous worshipers of Hanspur may twist or completely fabricate these messages so as to better manipulate their flock, but it seems Hanspur cares little about how his followers interpret his will.

Followers of Corosbel, in an attempt to discredit Hanspur's faith in civilized lands, have taken to murdering river travelers in the name of Hanspur while masquerading as members of his faith. Many of Hanspur's faithful are unfortunately unaware of this duplicity; some of his more superstitious followers have mistakenly taken up the practice in the belief that such a macabre offering protects them from the dangers of river travel.

TEMPLES AND SHRINES

The majority of Hanspur's devoted travel frequently, so there are few stationary temples to his faith. Most temples to Hanspur are aboard rafts or barges, while smaller floating shrines containing lit candles, coins, and other offerings are simply set adrift on river currents. Some riverside settlements feature altars to Hanspur outside their city gates or near wharves and docks, typically consisting of driftwood and reeds bound with rope into the effigy of a man. When multiple worshipers of Hanspur congregate, they use these holy sites as meeting places, sharing news and knowledge along with their perspectives on Hanspur's teachings. These moots are sometimes the only instance where one priest of Hanspur will ever meet another, and debate can become quite lively.

The largest temple devoted to Hanspur lies on the northern shore of Kallas Lake between the River Kingdoms and Kyonin. This house of worship is a flotilla of barges and rafts lashed together and anchored to form a floating island. The most dedicated followers of Hanspur congregate here irregularly to interpret visions and signs from the Water Rat.

A PRIEST'S ROLE

Priests of Hanspur are partially protectors and partially enforcers. Hanspur asks his faithful to guard river travelers on their journeys, but only from unnatural hazards such as river pirates or brigands. The faithful of Hanspur see environmental dangers as expected parts of the natural cycle, and many river travelers have found their end at the hands of vicious native predators while priests of Hanspur looked on. The sole exception to this rule is drowning, which Hanspur's priests will more often than not attempt to prevent.

Though most of Hanspur's followers are clerics, druids, and rangers, cults of Hanspur frequently indoctrinate hunters, rogues, shamans, slayers, and the occasional warpriest, as well. The fractious nature of Hanspur's religion ensures that there are no true archetypal structures of the Water Rat's faith. Hydrokineticists in the River Kingdoms often find worship of Hanspur a particularly profound calling. Some witches claim to be direct servants of Hanspur, particularly those with death, vengeance, or water patrons.

Priests of Hanspur view dusk as a sacred time of day, believing it to be either the hour of Hanspur's mortal death or the moment of his divine resurrection, depending on the particular tenets of a given sect. During the hour of dusk, the faithful of Hanspur isolate themselves and sit in quiet contemplation near or in a river. When a river is not immediately accessible, his priests seek out some source of water in which to douse themselves. A priest of Hanspur usually ends his dusk worship with a moment of simulated drowning, either by briefly submersing himself in an available river, or by pouring water over his face with a cloth over his eyes. Following this ritual, he prepares his spells while contemplating his god's final moments as a mortal, attempting to understand the mystery of how a death transitioned into divinity and the power therein. (This counts as the priest's obedience.)

Beyond protecting river travelers, some of Hanspur's priests concern themselves with the activities of the daemonic harbinger Corosbel. While few of Hanspur's faithful have even an inkling of

their god's history with the harbinger, Hanspur's clerics and warpriests sometimes receive visions directing them to confront cabals of Corosbel's faithful and slaughter the daemon's followers to the last. Corosbel's twisting of Hanspur's faithful has confused this mission, however, leading clerics and warpriests of Hanspur to sometimes kill members of their own faith.

Druids and rangers who venerate Hanspur are entrusted with magic that allows them to better navigate the hazards of the rivers. Such druids can prepare *water walk* as a 3rd-level spell. Rangers devoted to Hanspur add *water breathing* to their spell list as a 2nd-level spell so as to not suffer the same fate as Hanspur himself.

ADVENTURERS

Any who respect the power and influence of rivers are welcome to join Hanspur's faithful. Although he is most venerated by Kellid and Varisian worshipers, there is no clear ethnic delineation among his followers. Likewise, Hanspur's faith has no obvious doctrine regarding morality. While some sects of Hanspur see themselves as good-hearted travelers living free on the river, protecting those who cannot protect themselves, there are just as many cruel adherents who manipulate and exploit travelers. Hanspur cares only that his followers appreciate and accept freedom and do not impose needless laws or restrictions upon others. Freedom, ultimately, is the sole unifying tenet of Hanspur's faith.

Adventurers who worship Hanspur sometimes carry the Water Rat's will beyond the boundaries of the River Kingdom, extending his influence to foreign waterways. It is these adventurers who are most likely to be tasked with hunting down agents of the daemonic harbinger Corosbel across Golarion. They take up Hanspur's own mantle as both guardian and vigilante, protecting the people of waterways and rivers while punishing those who would take advantage of river travelers.

CLOTHING

Hanspur's faithful do not have a uniform style of dress, though many work Hanspur's colors—blue and gold—into their attire. Most priests of Hanspur dress in accordance with local cultures or wear garb suitable for river life and travel. Short pants, waterproof ponchos, wide-brimmed hats, and the like are all common. Kellid and Varisian worshipers of Hanspur tend to incorporate tattoos into their attire, and Varisians weave curvy, flowing patterns into their kapenias. Clerics and warpriests of Hanspur prefer to wear armor that does not impede swimming.

HOLY TEXT

Hanspur's religious text includes homilies about life and death on the river, as well as inspirational adages regarding freedom and self-sufficiency that provided the basis for the Six River Freedoms doctrine—the closest thing the River Kingdoms have to a national code of laws. Each priest of Hanspur adapts and modifies these texts according to her personal outlook on Hanspur's faith. These variations only deepen the mystery surrounding Hanspur's faith and origin.

HOLIDAYS

Hanspur's faith has no organized holidays. Instead, his worshipers attend dedication ceremonies of river-going vessels to bless them for safe passage and take great delight in communities that build ships, thus increasing river traffic. Every sect of Hanspur has a day devoted to his death and another to his resurrection, though the exact timing of these holidays varies from sect to sect. Most priests of Hanspur celebrate his death as one might a momentous accomplishment, while the date assigned to Hanspur's resurrection is honored with song and contemplative retrospection. Ratfolk followers of Hanspur celebrate only his death, believing that this was the moment Ashkaelae ascended.

APHORISMS

Hanspur's aphorisms are largely taken from the Six River Freedoms and combined with quotes misattributed to historical figures, borrowed from other religions, or made up by Hanspur's faithful, such as the following.

Say What You Will, I Live Free: Taken directly from the Six River Freedoms, this maxim refers to the freedom of speech enjoyed by residents of the River Kingdoms. To the followers of Hanspur, this aphorism is often used when confronted with the conflicting views of a different priest of Hanspur. The saying is used to defuse arguments by celebrating the diversity of opinion and belief that Hanspur affords his faithful.

RELATIONS WITH OTHER RELIGIONS

Hanspur's clandestine war with the daemonic harbinger Corosbel consumes much of the Water Rat's attention, and he extends this animosity toward all of the daemonic harbingers and the Horsemen, making a point of thwarting their goals whenever the opportunity arises. Hanspur views Gozreh as an enigmatic parental figure, both because of Gozreh's involvement in continuing Hanspur's existence, and also because of prior associations from the time of his mortal life. This fascination is not often reciprocated by Gozreh. Followers of the two beings are casual acquaintances at best, with their domains infrequently overlapping. Hanspur's relations with Pharasma are lukewarm, and though he helps in protecting the River of Souls, the goddess sees Hanspur's return to life from death as an affront, albeit a minor one.

Beyond the gods venerated in the River Kingdoms, Hanspur has a strained relationship with the Osiriani river goddess Wadjet. While the two gods each claim specific rivers as their domains, wandering priests of Hanspur have, on occasion, clashed with priests of Wadjet while visiting the River Sphinx. As a lawful good deity, Wadjet rejects Hanspur's capricious nature and sees his priests as a plague on her river; she seeks to force his priests to obey her laws while they travel her waters.

Because of the proximity of their planar domains, Hanspur and Besmara share an unusual relationship with one another. The Pirate Queen and the Water Rat have little in common personally, but each has aided the other on matters of personal significance as a measure of unusual camaraderie between free spirits. Besmara occasionally allows him aboard her ship, *Seawraith,* for joint attacks on daemons in service to Corosbel, and

Hanspur has spent time raiding the planes at Besmara's side. Though these dalliances do not last long, they are reflected in the easy interactions between their respective followers. Hanspur and Gyronna share a grudging respect based on their shared origins as Kellids.

Hanspur's relations with other gods are handled on a largely case-by-case basis, as he has no strong historical enmity against or alliances with them.

REALM

Hanspur's divine realm is a circuitous system of rivers that stretches across the whole of the Maelstrom. These waterways twist and divide without rhyme or reason, never staying in the same place for long. Because of his divine status and enmity towards daemons, Hanspur claims a portion of the infamous River Styx as his own, and harries daemons that attempt to cross his domain. The notable exception to this treatment are the thanadaemons that ferry travelers safely across the Styx; Hanspur respects these beings in spite of their daemonic nature.

PLANAR ALLIES

Hanspur's divine servants are all creatures born of rivers or entities that have returned after death. Hanspur often calls on the service of water elementals to do his bidding, though some of his more powerful agents noted below can be called using spells such as *planar ally.*

Ashkaelae's Brood (herald of Hanspur): Hanspur's herald is not a single entity, but rather an enormous unique swarm of waterlogged rats that move with a single mind. These voracious creatures surge and crash like a wave of flesh, shrieking and crying as they do. Sometimes these sounds rise to a crescendo, calling out in a voice that is composed of many but speaks as one. These rats are believed to be the many children of Ashkaelae, Hanspur's rat companion. Unlike ordinary rats, Ashkaelae's Brood do not carry diseases or parasites, and can both swim easily and breathe underwater. Hanspur sends Ashkaelae's Brood as a messenger when his will must be expressly stated or, more frequently, as a punishment when one of his followers egregiously violates Hanspur's few tenets.

The Lost Ferryman (CN unique thanadaemon): When Hanspur ascended and claimed his divine realm, he took a portion of the River Styx as part of that dominion, and confronted the Lost Ferryman, a thanadaemon plying that river at the time. While the newly reborn god intended to destroy the daemon out of spite, the Lost Ferryman was able to convince Hanspur of his worth and the importance of free travel down the Styx, citing his kind's unique capacity for navigating that river's treacherous waters. Hanspur considered the daemon's words and stole him from the Horseman of Death to act as ferryman of the Styx in his own domain.

Kurgess

Kurgess, the Strong Man, was once a mortal of peerless physical prowess. As legends of his sporting victories and his noble death spread across the Inner Sea region—and even other planes—athletes began looking to Kurgess as a role model, and competitions were often dedicated to him as the embodiment of honor and athleticism. Shortly thereafter, Cayden Cailean and Desna raised Kurgess to godhood, crowning him with deific powers. Why they did this remains up for debate, but more than a few scholars whisper that Kurgess might actually be the two deities' half-mortal son. He stands as patron of and inspiration for all who engage in physical challenges.

THE STRONG MAN

God of bravery, competition, and sports

Alignment NG

Domains Community, Good, Luck, Strength, Travel

Subdomains Agathion, Family, Fate, Home, Resolve, Trade

Favored Weapon javelin

Centers of Worship Andoran, Druma, Isger, the Shackles, Taldor

Nationality Taldan

Obedience Find the nearest boulder, log, or other unattended object that you can reliably lift over your head, and hold it up high for the duration of the obedience while meditating on the ennobling nature of sports and tests of physical might. If you are interrupted at any time by any creature or person, you must challenge your interrupter to a contest of strength, speed, or stamina, with the boulder or another object of your obedience used as the main focus of the competition. Regardless of who wins, you gain a +2 sacred bonus on Acrobatics and Climb checks.

> As healthy competition is your meal, so is fairness and honor your wine, for one without the other is dry and bitter indeed.
>
> —Catalog of Champions

EVANGELIST BOONS

1: Blessed Runner (Sp) *longstrider* 3/day, *cat's grace* 2/day, or *haste* 1/day

2: Strong One (Su) You are wise enough to know that strength is a useful attribute for more than just competition and combat, and Kurgess smiles upon you for this wisdom, granting you greater strength for your everyday activities. You gain a +2 sacred bonus on all Strength-based skill checks.

3: Farmer's Brawn (Su) Great strength finds those who need it most, granting even the weakest individuals near-supernatural abilities in moments of panic or to rescue loved ones, and Kurgess's evangelists are especially prone to such instantaneous bursts of brawn. Treat your carrying capacity as though your Strength ability score were 3 points higher than it actually is. Once per day, as long as you are wearing light, medium, or no armor, you can lift up to two unconscious or dead Medium or smaller creatures and their equipment onto your shoulders and still move up to your base speed, ignoring the added weight of your fallen comrades. You cannot both attack and move in the same round while carrying one or more creatures in this way. You can carry your companions in this way for a number of rounds equal to your Hit Dice; afterward, they encumber you as normal.

EXALTED BOONS

1: Holy Strength (Sp) *enlarge person* 3/day, *bull's strength* 2/day, or *rage* 1/day

2: Coordinated Escape (Su) You and your allies know it is better to flee and live to continue the fight another day than to die honorable deaths that accomplish nothing. Three times per day as a standard action, you can shout an inspirational command that affects you and any allies within 60 feet for a number of rounds equal to your Hit Dice. During this time, affected characters can use the withdraw action to move up to triple their base speed (instead of up to double their base speed).

3: Break the Anvil (Su) You don't believe it is enough to shame your enemies by relieving them of their weapons—if possible, you must shatter those weapons so they can never again stand against you. Once per day, you can perform a disarm or sunder combat maneuver with a +4 competence bonus against an adjacent creature and a weapon it holds. If you succeed, the creature's weapon is simultaneously damaged and disarmed, as though you had succeeded at both combat maneuvers simultaneously. If you exceed the target's Combat Maneuver Defense by 10 or more, the target drops the items it is carrying in both hands, but you only sunder the weapon you initially targeted. If you don't have either the Improved Disarm or Improved Sunder feat or a similar ability, this attempt provokes attacks of opportunity as normal; however, if you have one of the feats or a similar ability, this attempt does not provoke attacks of opportunity.

SENTINEL BOONS

1: Master of Games (Sp) *true strike* 3/day, *bear's endurance* 2/day, or *heroism* 1/day

2: Reveal Frauds (Sp) Like Kurgess, your keen sense of honor will not allow you to brook cheats among your ranks, and the insight bestowed by your devotion to your ideals has taught you to spot a fraud based on a hunch. You can use *discern lies*, as per the spell, for a number of rounds per day equal to your Hit Dice. These rounds need not be consecutive. Activating this ability is an immediate action.

3: Unchained Savior (Su) You are nothing without your teammates, and are willing to sacrifice your own safety to keep them alive. Once per day as an immediate action, if an ally within 60 feet of you would normally take enough damage to fall unconscious or die, you can move to an adjacent space and intercept the killing blow, taking the damage in your ally's place. If the attack would have inflicted any effects other than hit point damage, those effects are negated. If the damage would bring you to negative hit points, you are brought to 0 hit points instead, and the remaining damage is negated. Any attacks of opportunity you provoke by moving in this way are resolved after you take the damage from the intercepted blow; you take any damage from those attacks as normal.

KURGESS'S PALADIN CODE

Paladins of Kurgess are jovial in nature but firm in conviction, and brook no cheaters or liars among their ranks. Their tenants include the following affirmations.

- Fairness and good sportsmanship are testaments to one's virtue. I must set the finest example of what it means to be sporting and noble in challenges of strength and honor.

- A challenge that is won unfairly is not a challenge won. I am no cheat, and I will lose any contest of brawn, honor, or mettle rather than resort to knavery or trickery.

- Frauds have no place among true competitors. In contests of import and high-stakes trials, I will unrelentingly reveal the untruthful and deliver them to their proper justice.

- Winning and losing are two sides of the same coin, and both are worthy of acknowledgment. I treat champions with respect, but honor losers for their courage and willingness to challenge themselves.

- I respectfully seek tutelage from my betters, give honest guidance to the less accomplished, and cherish most of all my friendships with rivals whose skill matches my own.

- Every day is a contest to better oneself, and every deed undertaken is an opportunity to condition my allies and myself for the trials ahead.

UNDERSTANDING KURGESS

About 300 years ago, Kurgess was merely a strapping farm boy from Taldor, and his mortal life is well-documented. Born to unknown parents, Kurgess was abandoned as an infant upon the doorstep of a Taldan couple who took him in. His extraordinary strength manifested before he even reached puberty—by the age of eight, he could pull a sleigh loaded with his brothers and sisters back and forth across a field all afternoon. One day, Kurgess spotted a traveling merchant on the road who had gotten his carriage stuck in a ditch. The selfless youth shook hands with the stranger before disconnecting the carriage from its train and heaving the entire vehicle out of the ditch unaided. Impressed by the boy's wondrous brawn, the merchant extended an offer: Kurgess could join him in his travels, and together they would roam Taldor, with Kurgess competing in contests of strength and speed. By the time Kurgess turned 20, he was packing stadiums with peasants as well as aristocrats eager to see the so-called Strong Man best time-honored champions at their own games. Unfortunately, Kurgess's vast talent and good-natured sportsmanship earned him the jealousy and bitterness of many of his more unscrupulous rivals.

Kurgess's final act as a mortal took place at the third annual Raptor Run in Taldor's capital of Oppara. Before the competition, Kurgess's enemies laid down a vicious trap for the Strong Man and any competitors unfortunate enough to be riding alongside him. Kurgess caught wind of the scheme and sacrificed himself, crashing his chariot onto the trap and saving the other athletes. When the clerics pronounced the gladiator dead, the entire city mourned for the champion, and Kurgess became a martyr.

THE CHURCH

The church of Kurgess is first and foremost dedicated to the pursuit of good sportsmanship and athletic achievements. Kurgessans believe that strength of body and character is the key that opens the gates to Nirvana, and train day in and day out to emulate the magnificent victories and honorable deeds of their god. In addition to participating in sporting events and competitions, followers of Kurgess donate their time and muscles to good causes such as aiding the ill, building homes, and performing acts of kindness for any strangers they encounter.

Most of Kurgess's devotees pursue a roaming lifestyle that mirrors their god's legendary travels, chasing competitions and contests all across Avistan and Garund. Whenever Kurgessans worship or win an important personal competition at a significant site, they leave their marks by hanging gilded chains from high rafters, tall spires, or otherwise seemingly unreachable places. This practice has inspired an unspoken tradition across southern Avistan: when a Kurgessan sees one of the telltale golden chains left by a previous adherent, the latest arrival does her best to climb, jump, or otherwise mount the obstacle and reach the chain, so she can add one of her own links to it. Heavily trafficked shrines can see dozens of traveling Kurgessans each year, and the most hallowed sanctuaries of the Strong Man bear golden chains hundreds of feet long.

Members of Kurgess's church generally fall into three categories, which are recognized by all members of the faith: champions, heralds, and laity. Champions are the most numerous among Kurgess's devoted—these are the brawlers, strongfolk, and athletes who embody Kurgess's strength and seek to follow in his divine footsteps. Officiates, priests, and other servants of the church who don't actually participate in physical competitions are called heralds—they are responsible for coordinating sporting events, maintaining the church and training grounds, and serving as squires for their champions in the arena. Least numerous are the laity, or lay worshipers—the common (and often destitute) farmers and artisans who make food and equipment for champions and heralds and rely heavily on the church's charity.

Unlike worshipers of other gods of battle who may revel in the bloodshed of their enemies, Kurgessans take little pleasure in mortal combat, and are hesitant to rush into war or prolonged political conflicts. Worshipers of Kurgess enjoy performing heroic acts for the less fortunate and are willing to reveal their true strength on the battlefield, but they are primarily a light-hearted lot who would prefer to train their bodies and play games in a world of peace rather than fight.

TEMPLES AND SHRINES

The largest Kurgessan temples—mostly in Taldor, though several have been built elsewhere—are broad stone structures held up with iron pillars gilded in gold. Blacksmiths, armorers, and farriers convene near these temples, crafting gold-colored ceremonial armor for the evangelists who spread the Strong Man's gospel through sports and charity. Temples to Kurgess are nearly always built next to stadiums, coliseums, and arenas; sometimes they are part of those structures themselves. When they aren't, sacred halls typically connect the church to its adjacent sporting ground, allowing adherents of the Strong Man to easily find their way to their next sparring match after prayer or return to the temple after a long day of wrestling. Smaller or poorer temples typically occupy single stone buildings in settlements where sports are less celebrated.

A PRIEST'S ROLE

Like all members of the church, Kurgessan priests are often wanderers. They journey across southern Avistan and beyond, scouring the globe for honorable competitions (in the case of priests who compete) or worthy athletes to convert to the faith and sponsor in future contests. Sponsorship is a great responsibility for Kurgessan priests, and one not to be taken lightly.

The few priests of Kurgess who adopt settled lifestyles tend to practice their faith by committing energy to charities, organizing sporting events to draw visitors to town, and training militia groups to defend their settlements and eradicate monsters. As an orphan himself, Kurgess smiles down on those who help youths from unfortunate backgrounds.

The hardiest Kurgessan priests wear thick iron bangles, anklets, and leather vests lined with iron tablets that can weigh upward of 100 pounds. Such zealots train daily while wearing weighted garb, honing their bodies against the added weight until it is practically a second skin. When the time comes to finally put their training to the test, these disciples shed their self-imposed burdens, their muscles so unrestrained they practically fly into the fray.

"Honor, fairness, and above all, respect"—this is Kurgess's dogma. Kurgessan priests love the thrill of a win, but they also know the value of bittersweet losses, seeing victory and defeat as closely intertwined. So too do these revelers understand that in order to claim glory,

one must do so graciously; a boastful winner is no winner at all, and sore losers create mental and spiritual baggage that only weighs them down during the next match. Of course, in mortal combat, the niceties of sportsmanship and good manners are set aside so that a Kurgessan can protect herself and her allies. Clerics of Kurgess can prepare *expeditious retreat* and *jump* as 1st-level spells.

ADVENTURERS

Performing acts of good, finding new competitors to best, and rooting out the unjust are all vital aspects of Kurgess's ethos, and they make for a good adventuring lifestyle as well. What's more, over the last 300 years, there have been rumors of Kurgess himself appearing in mortal guise to take part in sporting events. It is said that he equally protects and encourages his fellow competitors while

doing so. This has led to a gradual expansion of his faith, and consequently, of the number of adventurers who count themselves among his followers.

It isn't in a Kurgessan's nature to stay in one place for too long. Devotees seek to emulate their god's accomplishments by leading a nomadic life in order to compete in as many matches, spars, and tournaments as they can in their lifetimes.

CLOTHING

In life, Kurgess was famous for wearing sparse attire and eschewing civilized garb. In turn, Kurgess's adherents prefer humble gladiatorial gear such as short togas, cloth pants or wrappings, and loincloths. This clothing is often held together with small golden chains. Officiates of the Strong Man usually wear tabards or togas bearing their

god's holy symbol. Of course, clothing standards tend to fall by the wayside in the heat of sports, and adherents focus more on comfort and ease of mobility than modesty.

HOLY TEXT

The following work of text features prominently among Kurgess's canon.

Catalog of Champions: This exhaustive record contains a preamble on the philosophy behind sportsmanship and noble competition, as well as names the winners of a variety of contests, physical tests, and sporting events held around the Inner Sea region and beyond. Along with the champions' names, each entry includes the rules of the sport, mythological stories behind the sport, and the time, weight, or act one must best to claim a spot on the list of champions. While normally recorded on vellum scrolls, several versions of this ancient record are inscribed on the stones of notable coliseums such as Valknar Gladiatorial College in the River Kingdom of Tymon and the pillars that line the Lionsgate district in Oppara.

HOLIDAYS

Worshipers of Kurgess celebrate the following holidays.

Carnival of Kurgess: Named after the Strong Man, the Carnival of Kurgess is a week-long competition of gladiatorial games and contests held on Widowmaker Isle in the Shackles once every 2 years. While most of the matches are not to the death, the mortality rate of contestants is still high due to the brutal nature of the events and the contest's magnificent grand prize—the title of Mayor of Widowmaker Isle. The celebration of this holiday is a point of contention for some Kurgessan priests, who find the carnival organizers too bloodthirsty for their tastes.

Running of the Raptors: Also known as Raptor's Run, this event is held each year in the streets of Lionsgate in Oppara. Participants must race through the emptied roads dodging obstacles and hurdles while being chased by a freed pack of raptors. The mortal Kurgess died to save the other participants of the third Running of the Raptors, so this event bears special significance for the Strong Man's Taldan disciples. Adherents use the occasion to celebrate Kurgess's life as well as his mission; in recent years, Kurgessans who win the event have started giving their winnings to poor or fledgling orphanages around Taldor.

APHORISMS

Kurgessans frequently call upon the strength of their god in contests as well as battles, and the following aphorisms succinctly represent their ethos.

The Heat of Sports, the Winds of Nirvana: Kurgessans ascribe many of the body's natural responses to physical exertion to a divine connection with sites on Nirvana, home of the Strong Man's domain. Perspiration is a cooling fog rolling across Kurgess's Field, a quickened pulse comes from the pounding of waterfalls at the Skyward Cliffs, and an increase in body temperature signifies that one is channeling winds from the Dreaming Sun Volcano.

I Always Fight Again: A bitter defeat is only the end of one's journey if one allows it to be. Even Kurgess occasionally lost a match (though the circumstances of such losses were always dubious), and had it not been for his final defeat, he would have never risen to godhood.

RELATIONS WITH OTHER RELIGIONS

While other gods associated with strength such as Cayden Cailean and Gorum draw worshipers similar to those of Kurgess, the Strong Man's faith is unique in that its adherents prize sportsmanship and good games above revelry or the rush of battle. Irorans share Kurgessans' appreciation for physical mastery and the thousands of hours of training that go into such pursuits, but that's where their similarities end. Irori's monks disdain Kurgess's commitment to what they see as frivolous games, and Kurgessans regard Irorans' dedication to neutrality as an obstruction to the pursuit of a satisfying and virtuous life.

Cayden Cailean and Desna certainly lifted Kurgess from legend to godhood; what other feelings they have toward the Strong Man are debatable. Theologians and some priests of Kurgess speculate that at least one of them is Kurgess's parent, but the gods themselves have remained silent on the matter; still, adherents of Kurgess are welcomed with open arms in temples to Desna and Cayden Cailean alike. If the rumors about Kurgess's parentage were true, it would certainly explain the Strong Man's godly might as a mortal and the deities' decision to help raise their son to divinity.

As a Taldan mortal who made frequent trips to nearby Qadira, Kurgess found many good games and even brief love affairs with members of the Cult of the Dawnflower; members of the two religions similarly find much to enjoy about one another, as they share a common cause for good. Milani's devotees do not care as much for the games and sports to which Kurgessans commit their lives, but respect their comrades' dedication to self-sacrifice and helping others. Both faiths are common in areas where they are persecuted; by combining their efforts, these worshipers stand a far better chance of spreading their messages and overthrowing their oppressors.

Kurgessans cannot tolerate worshipers of destructive gods such as Norgorber or Rovagug, and rarely ally with their adherents. When working together is unavoidable due to an important common goal or exceptional circumstances, Kurgessans begrudgingly justify their unfortunate partnership by subtly showing off their strength and besting comrades in light-hearted contests in order to show the superiority of their god.

REALM

Kurgess resides on the plane of Nirvana, in an endless expanse of plains and rolling grasslands called Kurgess's Field. While strangers to the realm may find it eerie, natives tread the solemn grounds with reverence and respect. Massive circles of orange clay dot the region—sprawling arenas carved into the ground so wanderers can rest or challenge one another to good-natured bouts. Mortals who end up in Kurgess's Field after death happily congregate in otherworldly urban centers that host sporting and gaming festivals every day, where the sun always shines onto the countless coliseums, hippodromes, and stadiums made of iron and gold.

PLANAR ALLIES

Kurgess has many dedicated and loyal servants on Nirvana. The following otherworldly servants of the Strong Man can be called via *planar ally* or similar spells.

Exodor (unique advanced half-celestial riding horse): Legend has it that Kurgess found his magnificent steed, Exodor, in the Taldan highlands east of Zimar, and he tamed the wild stallion by living in the wilds alongside him through the winter. The golden-maned horse is a glorious sight with or without a rider, and Exodor is trained for combat as well as jousting and racing. Worshipers of Kurgess can also call upon Exodor's celestial descendants using spells such as *summon monster II*.

Marpitus, the Severed Chimera (unique mythic chimera): Villagers on the border between Taldor and Qadira still celebrate the mortal Kurgess's defeat of the mythic chimera Marpitus, which plagued farmers and travelers in the region for decades. Legend has it that Kurgess wrestled with Marpitus until the early morning hours, when he finally bested the beast and cut off its serpent-headed tail before landing the killing blow. When Kurgess ascended to godhood, he dredged up the soul of Marpitus from the underworld to act as his divine servant. The spirit of the Severed Chimera is still missing its venomous tail, and Kurgess's divine magic has ensured the tempestuous guardian serves his followers faithfully.

Watcher Surmios (herald of Kurgess): This unique astral deva is a loyal servant and friend of Kurgess. It was Surmios who witnessed Kurgess's grand self-sacrifice at the Third Running of the Raptors and led the champion's soul to Nirvana. When Cayden Cailean and Desna elevated Kurgess to godhood, Surmios stood by the Strong Man's side and vouched for his nobility and worthiness. The angel even accepted the honor of plunging his celestial sword into the chest of Kurgess's petitioner spirit to mark the beginning of the Strong Man's existence as a god. Now, Watcher Surmios descends to the mortal realm to assist and encourage followers of Kurgess as they pursue righteous causes or attempt to overcome impossible obstacles.

Milani

Milani knows that freedom, much like a rose, can flourish under almost any conditions, though it must occasionally be watered with the blood of martyrs. She embodies hope, devotion to a cause, and the will to rise up against oppression. The Everbloom is worshiped throughout Golarion as a protector-goddess and a hero to those suffering under the yoke of tyrants and slavers. She is not a deity who enjoys violence, but she and her followers are willing to fight and even die to break the shackles of despotism and injustice. Revolutionaries call upon her for protection, and those living in bondage pray to her for the courage to rebel and claim their freedom.

THE EVERBLOOM

Goddess of devotion, hope, and uprisings

Alignment CG

Domains Chaos, Good, Healing, Liberation, Protection

Subdomains Azata, Defense, Freedom, Purity, Restoration, Revolution

Favored Weapon morningstar

Centers of Worship Cheliax, Galt, Irrisen, Isger, Rahadoum

Nationality half-elf

Obedience Spend time meditating among roses you have planted yourself, so you can inhale their sacred scent while offering prayers to Milani. If no such roses are available, you can instead brew tea from herbs and rose petals and share the tea with close friends or neighbors. Preferred topics for conversation during this teatime include hopes for the future and preparations for times of need, but the act of sharing is itself enough. During times of war or conflict, though, you must instead spend time sparring, preferably with friends or neighbors whom you plan to fight alongside during the conflicts to come. If you are imprisoned and unable to spar, you can instead sing any song of hope or resistance in unison with one or more fellow prisoners. You gain a +2 sacred bonus on all saving throws against charm and compulsion effects, and a +2 sacred bonus on all rolls made to dispel or remove such effects from others.

> "You cannot compromise with evil or tyranny; you must rise up and fight for love, health, and life when they cannot be obtained peacefully."
>
> —The Light of Hope

EVANGELIST BOONS

1: Voice of the Everbloom (Sp) *command* 3/day, *enthrall* 2/day, or *suggestion* 1/day

2: Inspiring Presence (Su) Your mere presence bolsters your companions to fight harder in the face of even the most overwhelming odds and bolsters their hearts against growing weary of battle. Once per day as a standard action, you can provide all allies within 30 feet of you with a +1 sacred bonus on attack rolls, saving throws, and weapon damage rolls for a number of rounds equal to your Hit Dice.

3: Invoke Uprising (Sp) Even shackles of the mind do not escape your notice, and you can use an inspiring word from the teachings of Milani to help others find the strength to break those shackles. You are automatically aware of any creature within 10 feet of you that is currently under the effects of a charm, compulsion, or possession effect. Three times per day as a swift action, you can inspire such a creature to throw off the influence, granting that creature a new saving throw to immediately end the effect. If the effect does not normally allow a saving throw, calculate the save DC as normal if it is a spell; if it's not a spell, the DC is equal to 10 + 1/2 the source's Hit Dice + the source's Charisma modifier. The creature gains a sacred bonus on this saving throw equal to your Charisma bonus (minimum +1). This bonus is doubled if you include a physical touch as part of your invocation to rise up against the effect. In either case, this is a language-dependent effect.

EXALTED BOONS

1: Sacred Partisan (Sp) *divine favor* 3/day, *spiritual weapon* 2/day, or *magic vestment* 1/day

2: Alleyport (Sp) As the patron deity of urban uprisings, the Everbloom grants you the power to appear wherever in a settlement, dungeon, or other tight space you are most needed, or to escape to fight another day. Once per day as a swift action, you can teleport as per *dimension door*, but only when you are in an area no wider than your space, and you can arrive in only an area of similar width.

3: Wall of Roses (Sp) You can call upon Milani's symbolic roses to defend the innocent and the righteous while stymieing oppressors and their minions. Once per day, you can cast *wall of thorns*. The wall consists of a dense tangle of roses through which you and other worshipers of Milani can pass with ease.

The wall of roses heals from damage dealt to it at a rate of 5 hit points per round; it is immune to fire damage; and all piercing damage it deals bypasses damage reduction as if it were a good, magic, and silver weapon. Evil and lawful creatures damaged by a wall of roses automatically become sickened for the next minute (this is a poison effect).

SENTINEL BOONS

1: Neighborhood Guardian (Sp) *protection from evil* 3/day, *shield other* 2/day, or *magic circle against evil* 1/day

2: Stoic Guardian (Ex) Inspired by Milani's valor and steadfastness, you refuse to let magic corrupt your thoughts and deny fear any hold on your actions. You are immune to fear and charm effects, and gain a +4 sacred bonus on all saving throws against compulsion effects.

3: Martyrdom (Su) Your deeds and faith have earned you the Everbloom's blessing to give your life for a worthy cause and still fight on, and she shelters you in battle. As an immediate action once per day, whenever a single creature within 300 feet of you is slain by an effect or hit point damage, you can redirect that effect or damage onto yourself. You gain no saving throw to reduce effects redirected in this manner. If the effect kills you, you are restored to life in 1d4 rounds, as per *resurrection*, but once this resurrection effect occurs, you lose the ability to use martyrdom for 1 year.

MARTYRS REBORN

Milani's priests understand that a revolutionary's work is often rewarded with death, and they accept that they may one day be called to die for a cause. Fortunately, the goddess teaches that the truly devout who are martyred saving other people from death or tyranny will rise again in some way—perhaps even immediately, though being reborn in the faith is much more likely.

Some priests claim to be the incarnations of past followers of the goddess, able to access memories of past lives with the proper magic and meditation. A follower born after Milani ascended to godhood (about a century ago) can attempt to search for his past lives' memories by casting *legend lore*, which Milani grants only for this purpose to clerics, inquisitors, and warpriests as a 4th-level divine spell. The first time a caster attempts this use of the spell, he rolls 1d4–1 to determine the number of specific followers of Milani whose memories he accesses; each time he uses the spell, it reveals only information known to those individuals. If the result of the roll is 0, the caster can access no memories, either because he is not a reincarnated follower of Milani or because the goddess has not made his past lives' memories available.

UNDERSTANDING MILANI

Milani is relatively a new god, having ascended to full divinity only in the last century. Born a half-elf in a community of Forlorn elves over 2 millennia ago, Milani was raised to believe that the elves would one day return to restore true civilization to Golarion. When the demon Treerazer attacked Kyonin and the elves did not return to stop him, she embraced her human heritage and used her skills as a ranger to strike at Treerazer's minions. For this, the living god Aroden blessed her and tasked her with protecting isolated human settlements. As Aroden's champion, she famously defended the common folk against monsters, barbarians, oppressive lords, and diabolists for nearly a century. In reward for her service, Aroden sainted her and restored her youth. She spent the subsequent centuries crafting visions to inspire mortals to greatness. Upon Aroden's death, bearing a tiny portion of the Last Azlanti's power and maintaining part of his realm allowed her to gain a foothold on divinity.

Also known as the Everbloom, Milani is an outgoing goddess who still clearly remembers mortal life. Her religion is young and small enough for her to take a personal interest in the lives of her followers. Milani's ability to directly intervene in the mortal world is constrained, but she offers advice flavored with familiarity and jokes whenever she is able. She sees every object as a tool for fighting oppression, from a common scythe that can cut through binding ropes to a printing press than can subvert a tyrant's reputation. She also teaches that a common purpose makes the whole greater than the sum of the individual parts—whether that purpose is to start a revolution, drive out an unscrupulous lender, or just get through a rough spot in a marriage. A person must recognize and take advantage of her strengths, acknowledge and compensate for her faults, and push past despair to victory.

Milani manifests as a half-elven woman in the prime of life with stark white hair and white swan's wings. She is usually dressed as a ranger, clad in homemade light armor made of leather and wood, and she carries a morningstar and shield. In art, she is usually shown breaking chains, slaying fiends, and leading peasants to overwhelm evil-looking knights.

THE CHURCH

Most of Milani's worshipers are humans, but she has many half-elven and half-orc followers as well. Her priests are clerics or rangers; the rare inquisitor of Milani has no official role. A typical worshiper of Milani is a human commoner or expert who prefers a life of peace and freedom, but is willing to take up arms against evil when necessary. Her followers are optimistic, loving, friendly, and accepting, but not afraid to throw a punch (or take one) in response to an offense or injustice.

Milani's followers take their defensive responsibilities seriously; they know the history books are full of razed towns that allowed themselves to be overrun by invaders or crushed under the boots of a tyrant's enforcers. When training others to fight, they set aside any inclinations to joke or coddle, for soft words make weak soldiers.

During an uprising, the church welcomes those with skill at arms. Should personalities conflict during these times, the priests normally allow visitors to make their own plans for dealing with the problem. Priests also coordinate the rest of the community, preferably in a way that endangers as few innocent lives as possible.

The church is organized much like a cult, with small, independent cells able to function without communication from other communities, but willing to use whatever channels they have to coordinate efforts. The church puts little stock in grand ceremonies, medals, or titles, preferring to let talented leaders rise to the top on their own merits and expecting that other members of the faith will assist when needed.

Though Milani was born a half-elf, her church avoids elven culture (though not its role in her heritage). Instead, she and her faithful focus on the bright hearts and stubborn wills of the human race. Her church welcomes half-elves and half-orcs; many others of mingled blood who reject their non-human heritage see her as their patron—a symbol of the greatness that a mixed-race person can achieve despite prejudice. Additionally, some halflings venerate her for defending freedom and a few dwarves and gnomes sing her praises.

Services mix historical speeches, songs, and inspirational anecdotes about devotion and overcoming hardship. Temple music is folksy, and utilizes drums, simple stringed instruments, and singing. Many of her hymns double as revolutionary songs and are used as coded messages to listeners, warning of hostile patrols or members of the community who need help, or ridiculing current tyrants.

Milani greatly encourages her followers to find love and marry. As a mortal who outlived most of her human friends, she understands a widow's grief and teaches that finding love again after a spouse dies is normal and healthy. She does expect married couples to be true to each other, and has little sympathy for spouses who stray—if a partner has a wandering eye, better to end the marriage and find someone who wants only you than to wait for the inevitable pain of betrayal. She believes that children should be spared the horrors of war so they can grow up with loving hearts; using children or young people as soldiers is abhorrent to her.

Milani shows she is pleased through images of roses, the scent of roses, or the appearance of white animals (particularly doves, mice, and owls). When she's angered (usually by betrayal), flowers wither and sprout thorns, tiny wounds bleed excessively, and spilled liquids (especially drops of blood) form the shape of a rose.

TEMPLES AND SHRINES

Milanite temples are built on an incline, like a theater, so the speaker is at the bottom and the seats rise upward from that point. To leave the temple, followers must ascend from a low point, just as a person under the thumb of a tyrant must rise up. The lowest point is built at ground level, and beneath the inclined floor is a small and secret crawl space; in peacetime this is used to store supplies, and in periods of war it is used to hide weapons and freedom fighters. Most temples have a rose garden or at least a well-tended rose bush.

In smaller communities, a town hall may double as a temple, with a small shrine or altar kept out of the way or behind a curtain when not needed. Shrines to Milani are common in old Arodenite temples; even temples

that have since been converted to the worship of Iomedae often have a small alcove with rose iconography or a niche along the outer wall where a rose bush grows wild. In lands where her faith is suppressed, a site of worship may be little more than a head-sized rock with a rose carved near the bottom (or even hidden on the underside), or a small rosebush surrounded by a circle of smooth stones.

A PRIEST'S ROLE

Milani's priests are mainly clerics or rangers. In peacetime, her clerics usually divide their time between tending to the spiritual needs of the community and working at a standard profession, such as carpentry or leatherworking. Her rangers are border guards for communities, scaring off dangerous animals, hunting monsters, and capturing fleeing criminals. They greatly value individual freedom, but recognize that the community is stronger than the sum of its individuals, and even unpleasant civic measures such as (fair) taxes contribute to the betterment of society and the welfare of the common folk. Priests of Milani plan for the long term, setting aside tools, weapons, and emergency money just in case they need to build, smite, or buy something in haste.

Most priests are trained in Heal to care for their community and in Knowledge (history) in order to better remember the lessons of the past.

In times of revolution or war, both kinds of priests are strategists, scouts, spies, and militia commanders. They lend their expertise and powers to soldiers and commoners, using spells such as *imbue with spell ability* and a ranger's bond with companions to make their allies more effective. They prefer hit-and-run tactics and superior battlefield mobility. A Milanite priest feels comfortable leading others, not because he believes he is superior, but because he knows together they can tear down something they could not defeat alone. Her priests understand that there is a time for talk and a time for action, and that sometimes great sacrifices must be made to defeat evil without compromise. It is the priest's duty to draw the line in the sand, stoke the fires of courage, and be the sword that strikes the first blow so others see that the enemy can be hurt.

Clerics and rangers of Milani can prepare *coordinated effort*APG and *good hope* as 3rd-level spells; rangers can also prepare *remove fear* as a 1st-level spell and *imbue with spell ability* as a 3rd-level spell. Her inquisitors can learn *good hope* as a 3rd-level spell.

ADVENTURERS

Devout adventurers of Milani are alert for causes worth their time, attention, and sacrifice. Inveterate martyrs, they can sometimes be reckless with their own lives and are utterly devoted to helping any innocent in need. If no one nearby needs saving, then they usually figure that it is time to seek out new tyrants and gather tools and information useful in overthrowing them.

Many other adventurers embrace Milani out of a more measured dedication to hope and liberation, such as a commitment to overthrowing specific oppressors or slavers. Half-orc and half-elf adventurers sometimes worship her as a paragon of what they hope to become after proving themselves as members of human society; these adventurers tend to go out of their way to embrace impetuousness and sacrifice for their goals.

CLOTHING

Formal dress for Milanite clergy is a long white tabard with dark brown trim and a red rose in the center, which is worn only for ceremonies. The priest traditionally adds a decoration to the trim—typically a button or embroidered emblem—for each person in the community who died defending another. In most communities, this garment is passed down to successive leaders; a few have scores of decorations going back to the origin of the church, and the faithful treasure these items. Adventuring priests of Milani mark their tabards or cloaks more informally to commemorate fallen allies, cohorts, or even animal companions. A priest or devout adventurer who wants to display her faith in more everyday settings might wear a badge or belt buckle with a rose emblem.

HOLY TEXT

It is customary to use a pressed rose as a bookmark in a Milanite holy text and, when giving a copy as a gift, to mark personally significant pages with individual rose petals.

The Light of Hope: The official book of the church begins as a history of Milani's deeds as a mortal, supposedly written by her after she became a saint. It also includes homilies about family, defense, hope, and perseverance, and a few ritual prayers and songs. In some communities it is split into two books, one focusing on her history and the other on her specific lessons for mortals.

HOLIDAYS

Individual Milanite communities celebrate anniversaries of patriotic war victories achieved with the help of civilian uprisings. The church also observes a moment of silence on the death anniversaries of local heroes. However, Milani's church does not celebrate All Kings Day, for Milani hates the endless violence wrought by Galt's Red Revolution.

Armasse: Celebrations of the Arodenite holiday of Armasse include teaching commoners to fight.

Even-Tongued Day: The faith celebrates freedom from Imperial Taldor on this day.

Foundation Day: On this day, the church observes a moment of silence for Aroden, who sainted Milani.

Liberty Day: The church in Andoran celebrates an uprising achieved with surprisingly little violence.

APHORISMS

As Milani's followers are ordinary people pushed into extraordinary circumstances, many of the faith's common phrases are used to inspire hope and determination.

Find Your Hidden Strength: The faithful understand that sometimes they must endure hardship to reach a better place. Milani teaches that humanity is at its very best when things are at their worst, and hope—courage of the heart—is a source of incredible power.

Know What Is Worth More Than Yourself: True devotion is the willingness to make sacrifices in order to protect something other than yourself. Whether this is a spouse, a child, your home, or freedom, by accepting responsibility for the things you love, you are given the choice to give up something to promote a greater good.

Peace, Love, Health, and Life: Also known as the "Four Pillars," these define the core of humanity's gifts. The cost of any action should be weighed against these ideals—promoting one at the cost of another might be worthwhile if the rewards outstrip the costs.

RELATIONS WITH OTHER RELIGIONS

Milani gets along well with most good gods, especially Cayden Cailean, a fellow ally of freedom; Desna, a hope-affirming goddess; Erastil and Torag, protectors of communities; Iomedae, a fellow servitor of Aroden; and Shelyn, the inspiration for perfect devotion. She is also friendly toward Kurgess, a deity with rural origins and a willingness to help others in need.

Milanites seek to build a quiet camaraderie with the faithful of other good gods, especially gods who are friendly with Milani. While the church of Milani generally has very modest resources, these allied faiths are often willing to provide support for their noble causes. The greater resources of other religions often prove the deciding factor that allows agents of the Everbloom to successfully fund a rebellion or arm defenders against a rising tyrant. Milani opposes slavery—even debt-based or voluntary slavery—which puts her church into conflict with many people in countries such as Katapesh and Qadira.

The Everbloom uses her position as a less-worshiped goddess to her advantage, avoiding attention from—and conflicts with—evil gods, except under circumstances in which she can aid mortals to thwart the plans of her opponents. Asmodeus and Zon-Kuthon are her most frequent targets, for she despises everything they stand for, especially how they glorify their wickedness.

Milani instructs her faithful to hide their affiliation in regions where the churches of evil gods are strong. Milanites in such circumstances know that to declare themselves publicly would be to invite ostracism or execution, which would prevent them from eventually rebelling against those oppressors. They often covertly aid larger and stronger good churches in these regions.

REALM

Milani has two realms: a tiny one carved out of Aroden's former realm in Axis, and one she has recently established in Elysium as a home more suited to her chaotic and goodly nature. Milani's Garden, her Elysian realm, is dominated by maze-like fortresses of beautiful rose bushes, and is where she spends most of her time. After Aroden's death, she created a defensible perimeter near the center of his collapsing realm, ultimately reforging those few square miles as her own divine realm, called the Refuge of the Red Rose.

PLANAR ALLIES

Most of Milani's divine servants are dead mortals granted sainthood, and most of those are human rangers with celestial heritage, veterans of many battles in life and after. Her most frequently conjured servitors are the following, and can be summoned with spells such as *planar ally.*

Charl (celestial human ranger): This sandy-haired, sturdy young man is eager to visit the mortal world and lend his expertise to the common folk. He wields a pair of old hunting knives or a homemade shortbow. He is a 6th-level ranger and prefers payment in the form of small stone magic items or gems.

Courage Heart (herald of Milani): This unique outsider (*Pathfinder Adventure Path #68: The Shackled Hut* 84) has two missions: to attack the powerful enemies of Milani's church—especially undead who would subjugate the common folk, and conjured outsiders used to strike fear into mortal hearts—and to inspire hope among mortals with the strength to turn against tyrants. Once a mortal ranger serving Milani, she was an early champion of Galt's Red Revolution when it deposed evil Chelish nobles. Later, when the movement become more about chaos and vengeance, she fought against it instead. She was executed as a Chelish sympathizer with a *final blade* that trapped her soul. Milani plucked the woman's soul from the artifact and made her a herald. Now the martyred hero keeps her original name secret so her living Galtan relatives do not become targets by association.

Dallem the Lucky (celestial human ranger): This waifish young woman has black hair except for a white stripe in the front. Quiet as a ghost, she loves teaching others how to move silently and incapacitate opponents without killing them. She is a 4th-level ranger and prefers being paid for her service with scrolls, sling bullets, and magic ointments.

Nyla (hound archon): Nyla is said to have been Milani's canine companion in life, granted sentience and immortality when the Everbloom became a goddess. The archon prefers her animal form—that of a white retriever—to her humanoid form, and enjoys using this shape to spy on enemies. She likes swimming and takes payment in the form of magical foods and potions.

Naderi

Initially a divine servitor of Shelyn, Naderi once nurtured the bonds between couples whose families, cultures, or societies forbade their love. She specialized in inspiring creative ways for them to express their affection in secret. She was particularly adamant about her belief that true love overcomes all obstacles, even death. However, when she appeared to a certain pair of star-crossed lovers, her impassioned words prompted them to jump from a waterfall right in front of her. As they tumbled, they gave thanks to Naderi, and the baffled servitor ascended to true divinity. Ever since, she has grappled with these events while remaining the patroness of forbidden love and romantic tragedy.

INTRODUCTION

ACHAEKEK

ALSETA

AVATI

BESMARA

EMIGH

ITARAK

GHLAUNDER

GROETUS

GYRONNA

HANSPUR

KURGESS

MILANI

NADERI

SIVANAH

ZYPHUS

THE LOST MAIDEN

Goddess of drowning, romantic tragedy, and suicide

Alignment N

Domains Charm, Nobility, Repose, Water

Subdomains Love, Lust, Martyr, Souls

Favored Weapon dagger

Centers of Worship Galt, Nidal, Qadira, Taldor, Ustalav

Nationality Taldan

Obedience Collect two unblemished white rose blossoms, open to their fullest but without any wilted petals. Stand beside a river and cut the blossoms from the stems, then set them on the water to float downstream. Meditate upon the beautiful perfection of love and the imperfection of a life that would deny it to star-crossed lovers. You gain a +2 profane or sacred bonus on Charisma-based skill checks. The type of bonus depends on your alignment—if you're neither good nor evil, you must choose either sacred or profane the first time you perform your obedience, and this choice can be changed.

EVANGELIST BOONS

1: Watery Souls (Sp) *wave shield*^ACG 3/day, *life pact*^ACG 2/day, or *water breathing* 1/day

2: Depths of the Maelstrom (Su) You do not fear death by water, for you are unafraid of your goddess's embrace, and you can capitalize on others' terror of the depths. Three times per day as an immediate action, when you step into any natural body of water, you can cause water within a 30-foot radius of where you stand to churn. You are unaffected by this churning. Any other creature wading or swimming in this water must attempt Swim checks as if the water were one category rougher; wading creatures must attempt DC 10 Swim checks, creatures swimming in calm water must make DC 15 Swim checks, creatures swimming in rough water must attempt DC 20 Swim checks, and creatures swimming in stormy water must attempt DC 25 Swim checks. If the water has a natural current, that current becomes fast moving. If the current was already fast moving, the DC of the Swim or Strength check to avoid going under increases to 15 + half your Hit Dice. This effect lasts for a number of rounds equal to your Hit Dice or until you leave the water, whichever is first.

3: Healing Waters (Su) You have learned that the waters can take life, but also that they can give it. Three times per day, you can hold a creature underwater for a number of rounds equal to half your Hit Dice. Each round, as long as the creature is submerged and holding its breath, it is healed of 1d8 + 5 points of damage. If the creature doesn't hold its breath, it doesn't receive healing that round. If you submerge a creature and heal it for fewer rounds than half your Hit Dice, it still counts as one use of this ability.

EXALTED BOONS

1: No Rest for the Living (Sp) *heightened awareness*^ACG 3/day, *compassionate ally*^UM 2/day, or *lover's vengeance*^ISWG 1/day

2: Nothing Left to Lose (Su) The losses you have suffered have made you morose and perhaps even aloof, but also fearless in battle. Once per day as a standard action, you may call out the name of a loved one you have lost. All opponents within hearing distance must succeed at a Will saving throw (DC = 10 + 1/2 your Hit Dice + your Wisdom modifier) or become shaken for a number of rounds equal to your Hit Dice. If you cause at least one creature to become shaken in this way, you gain a +2 profane or sacred bonus (of the same type as that provided by your obedience) on saving throws against spells with the mind-affecting descriptor for a number of rounds equal to your Hit Dice.

3: Final Strike (Sp) You can call down your goddess's cleansing wrath upon your wretched enemies. Three times per day as a standard action, you can cause a great column of white light to pour from the heavens that acts as a *fireball*, except the damage is force damage. A successful Reflex saving throw (DC = 13 + your Wisdom modifier) halves this damage.

SENTINEL BOONS

1: Frozen Despair (Sp) *icicle dagger*^UM 3/day, *castigate*^APG 2/day, or *howling agony*^UM 1/day.

2: All Who Live Suffer Loss (Su) You channel the despair and grief you have suffered into a cloud of sadness that saps the will of those who oppose you. All foes within a 30-foot, cone-shaped burst are staggered for a number of rounds equal to your Hit Dice, and take a –1 penalty on attack rolls, saving throws, ability checks, skill checks, and weapon damage rolls. A successful Will saving throw (DC = 10 + 1/2 your Hit Dice + your Charisma modifier) negates this effect.

3: Mantle of Tragic Grace (Sp) You drape yourself in tragic glamor, and your longing for rest puts you beyond the reach of mortal harm for a lingering moment. As a standard action, you can activate this mantle, which acts as a *globe of invulnerability*. You may use this ability for a number of rounds each day equal to your Hit Dice. These rounds do not need to be consecutive, and you can dismiss this effect as a standard action that does not provoke attacks of opportunity.

> O One of Eternal Purity, this world holds no mercy for us. Take us into your arms, where this anguish has no dominion, and our love will endure beyond death.
>
> —*The Seven Pangs of Longing*

NADERI AND SHELYN

Naderi's broken relationship with Shelyn remains a great source of pain to the Eternal Rose, a fact that further shames the younger goddess. This discomfort is reflected in the attitudes of the two goddesses' clergy. Shelyn's clergy members are determined to convince followers of Naderi that life holds too much beauty and wonder to leave behind, and that while romance is a great joy, an individual can have many true loves over a lifetime, both romantic and platonic, making no single loss worth dying for. Clergy of Naderi see worshipers of Shelyn as too shallow to understand the despair that comes of being denied the freedom to pursue a true love, though their goddess's respect for her former patron encourages them to avoid open criticism of Shelyn's faithful. Clergy members and lay worshipers of both goddesses are avid supporters of the arts. This tend to bring them into contact, though the focus on romantic tragedy insisted on by Naderi's followers exhausts Shelynites, and the Shelynites' attempts to get artists to focus on brighter and happier subjects irritates Naderi's worshipers. Overall, the more virtuous faithful of Naderi are natural allies to Shelynites, but the strained relationship between the goddesses and the morbid contemplation common to Naderi's worshipers tend to make members of the two faiths uneasy around one another.

UNDERSTANDING NADERI

Three centuries ago, as one of Shelyn's divine servitors, Naderi learned that a pair of lovers in Taldor who had long entreated the Eternal Rose for protection were quickly losing hope. She appeared in person to them in the mist of a great waterfall, affirming love's transcendence over mortal obstacles. Further, to hearten the lovers, she explained that love is one of the few bonds that sometimes endures beyond the end of mortal life, drawing souls together in the afterlife. To her shock, the young lovers took her words quite literally; they embraced and threw themselves into the falls, giving her thanks for showing them a way to truly be together at last.

This sacrifice propelled the dismayed Naderi—who had not intended to drive the lovers to their deaths—into godhood as the patron of suicide, especially for the cause of love. Her ascension burned away those elements of her nature not connected to this area of concern. Most forms of beauty ceased to touch her, though the beauty of love and the allure of tragic romance still called to her. Much of her capacity for true happiness was left behind as well, leaving her able to experience only bittersweet joy. Terrified of the changes she felt within herself, and believing she had betrayed Shelyn by accidentally turning two of her followers to her own worship and simultaneously driving them to suicide, Naderi fled Shelyn's realm.

Shelyn pursued, not out of anger, but out of concern, but Naderi eluded her. Over the centuries, the Eternal Rose has repeatedly attempted to reach Naderi, for she feels the Lost Maiden's nature gradually taking on a darker cast and is determined not to lose another loved one the way she lost her brother Zon-Kuthon. Meanwhile, the dark gods Urgathoa and Zyphus court Naderi, hoping to encourage the flowering of the more nihilistic side of her personality. Naderi herself remains a precariously balanced figure, clinging to the memory of the light and love and beauty she experienced as Shelyn's servitor, while struggling with a growing conviction that love is only ever consummated in death, and a burgeoning fascination with the aesthetics of suicide. She appears as a dark-haired young woman with large, haunted eyes, clad in waterlogged white garments and carrying a dagger.

THE CHURCH

Unlike the adherents of other neutral divinities, few people worship Naderi openly, or for a lifetime. Most of her faithful turn to her only as a last resort when they feel their love is doomed. Those left behind by a loved one's suicide may supplicate Naderi to care for the departed one—or, in anger at the abandonment, may beseech the goddess to bar the gates of her realm to the deceased, though such prayers are likely to be answered with signs of the goddess's displeasure. Naderi's secondary aspect as a goddess of drowning sometimes leads the parents of drowned children to beg her to shepherd their children's souls safely into the afterlife, after which they cast white flowers upon the waters in tribute. While this form of worship is seen as legitimate and practiced openly, it is far less common than worship of Naderi as patron of romantic suicide, which tends to be practiced in secret. Given the desperation of many of those who turn to her, and the stigma attached to suicide in most societies, Naderi has few dedicated clergy members, and even fewer organized congregations.

In addition to favoring her rare and scattered priests and priestesses, many of whom are survivors of suicide attempts or bereft lovers, Naderi sometimes grants spells to inquisitors. Such adherents track down and punish those who attempt to keep lovers apart or who maintain asylums and other institutions where those who wish to leave life behind are prevented from doing so.

Those few organized and public congregations of Naderi focus on providing memorials to the dead, maintaining the graves of those who died for love, and supporting artists who specialize in tragic romance. Most artists are glad for the patronage, though other artists and organizations that fund such endeavors look down on these offers, considering the projects to be morbid and overly florid. Naderi's congregations also come under fire from churches worshiping divinities that focus on freedom or justice. These critics point out that while Naderi's followers condemn laws, social institutions, and feuds that prevent young lovers from being together, they do nothing to eliminate them, instead choosing to extol the hollow virtue of devoting one's life—and often, death—to love.

Worship services usually involve hymns about love, readings or performances of romantic tragedies, and pledges of undying devotion between young lovers. If a couple requires a marriage ceremony conducted in secret, clerics of Naderi will happily provide it, even if the couple are not worshipers of the Lost Maiden, and the congregation is delighted to witness and help celebrate the clandestine union. Devotees of Naderi are also happy to hide and aid young couples fleeing the wrath of their parents or religious authorities, and take pride in their refusal to give up any information to such authorities—though their eagerness to relate their stories to others often results in information making its way back to the very people from whom the couple fled.

TEMPLES AND SHRINES

Naderi has few known temples, as her worshipers mostly meet in secret, if they bother to assemble at all. Scattered shrines to the Lost Maiden can be found near bodies of water, especially in areas where the desperate can easily drown themselves, such as ocean cliffs, waterfalls, high bridges, and the banks of rivers with strong undercurrents. Her worshipers sometimes turn grave sites and monuments built to commemorate those lost to suicide or drowning into altars to their goddess, though they often encounter resistance and anger from the families of the deceased, who object to the idea of celebrating their loved ones' deaths. Naderi's clergy members often maintain small sanctuaries in their homes; her few temples tend to be hidden in places where lovers gather clandestinely, such as sheltered groves, picturesque hilltops, and abandoned buildings. Popular places of worship are often unobtrusively marked with a white rose, magically preserved at the headiest moment of its bloom, a secret signal of devotion to Naderi known only to her faithful.

A PRIEST'S ROLE

Naderi's own ambivalence about her role and nature has led to a great deal of variation in how she is viewed. The most socially acceptable versions of her worship revolve around remembrance of those lost to drowning, and around support for lovers who cannot publicly express their bonds. These forms of worship are generally led by good clerics who focus on offering solace to bereaved families and safe places for persecuted lovers. In rare cases, they may help the devoted find painless deaths, though they reserve such aid for pairs in which one partner has a terminal illness and the other does not wish to go on alone, or to bereaved lovers unable to bear the pain of having lost their partners. In memory of Shelyn's role as Naderi's patron, a few such clerics also sneak into Kuthite temples to offer merciful deaths to those being tortured in Zon-Kuthon's name, feeding the victims an elixir that numbs their pain and gently stops their hearts. It also heals whatever wounds or deformities the Kuthites inflicted upon them, restoring the beauty of dignity to their bodies.

As Naderi's nature grows darker, her faith has also begun to attract less virtuous individuals. Some of her clerics are those who have been unlucky in love, longing for an ideal union but too damaged to believe it can exist between mortals. They encourage young lovers to heights of sentimental passion, teaching them to seek a moment of perfect love in which to die in one another's arms, explaining that mortal love is inherently imperfect and will inevitably disappoint unless it is made eternal at the instant of ultimate bliss. These more sinister priests work with couples to ensure they die in ways that leave them beautiful, so that when their bodies are found, they may inspire admiration and envy for the devotion they shared and the youthful loveliness with which they will be remembered.

Some clerics, like Naderi herself, attempt to remain balanced between virtue and corruption, giving shelter to persecuted lovers and comfort to those left behind by the death of a loved one, but also preaching that love is the only passion that endures beyond death, and that there is no shame in ending life at the height of its bloom.

A priest of Naderi begins her day by communing with

her goddess and praising the glory of romantic love. As a former divine servitor of Shelyn, goddess of beauty and the arts, Naderi still has a passionate appreciation for aesthetics, and most of her clerics are skilled writers, artists, or performers. They tend to spend much of their time writing romantic tragedies about doomed lovers, painting portraits of young couples in their final embraces, or performing songs and poems on similar themes.

Clerics of Naderi can prepare *lesser confusion* as a 1st-level spell, *crushing despair* as a 3rd-level spell, and *suffocation*[APG] as a 5th-level spell. Her inquisitors can also learn these spells at the same spell levels.

ADVENTURERS

Worshipers of Naderi adventure for many reasons, but most are driven in some way by the death of loved ones. Since her clerics are often survivors of suicide attempts or those who have lost lovers, many are eager to flee unhappy homes and even unhappier memories, yet those drawn to the goddess also struggle with a tendency to wallow in and romanticize their grief. These characteristics give them a haunted air, as if they are forever running from something they carry within themselves. At the same time, they often have intense empathy for others who grieve, and the wisest and best of them are able to transmute their own suffering into wisdom and comfort to offer others, even if they never find solace from their own sadness.

Bards, poets, and other artists are often drawn to Naderi as patron of tragic romance, and those who fancy themselves tragedians may worship her in that capacity. They may set out to investigate deaths involving young lovers, hoping to find inspiration for their next great work. Many lay worshipers of Naderi, however, are teenagers or young adults whose dramatic sentimentality makes them view the idea of dying for love as the highest form of romance. As they grow older and wiser, they tend to turn to the worship of other divinities.

A few lay worshipers are bereaved lovers or parents who have lost children to drowning. Such individuals may leave their homes to set the restless spirits of the deceased to rest or fulfill their last requests.

CLOTHING

Naderi's worshipers often hide their faith from their families and friends, fearing that those who care for them might attempt to turn them away from the Lost Maiden if they discovered their morbid romantic obsessions. Therefore, they don't normally wear any special clothing or tokens that might identify them. Those who have attempted suicide usually disguise any scars from their attempts except when meeting with Naderi's clerics or fellow adherents, to whom they reveal them proudly. When multiple worshipers gather, they may wear flowing red-and-blue garments that become heavy when waterlogged, in preparation for the day when they can drown themselves beautifully and surrender to their goddess's embrace.

HOLY TEXTS

Naderi's holy texts are poems, plays, and hymnals glorifying love and extolling the beauty of romantic tragedy.

The Lay of Arden and Lysena: The best known of Naderi's holy texts, this epic poem tells the story of the two young lovers whose deadly plunge down a waterfall sparked Naderi's ascension from divine servitor to goddess. Though most readers find it unbearably florid, the text is popular among teenage dreamers and sentimentalists, who pass tear-stained pages to their friends and quote passages to their sweethearts.

The Seven Pangs of Longing: These plays are the work of Rithallen, a Nirmathi playwright whose consuming romance with an unidentified Molthuni noblewoman known only as the Lily of Canorate inspired him to author a cycle of linked tragedies involving arranged marriages that separate young lovers.

HOLIDAYS

Naderi's church has few holidays, though worshipers commemorate the tragic deaths of lovers on a local level, placing votive candles, flowers, and portraits at the sites where young couples have met their ends.

Winterbloom: This universal holiday is the approximate anniversary of Naderi's ascension on 15 Kuthona. Celebrations are typically understated but include readings of *The Lay of Arden and Lysena*.

APHORISMS

Most of the pronouncements of Naderi's faithful are intended to comfort the bereaved, reassuring frightened young lovers that love is stronger than whatever persecution they face and insisting that, unlike other memories and emotions, love endures even after death.

Cut the Bloom at Its Height: Many of Naderi's faithful believe that if lovers die when their love is most perfect, they take that idealized passion with them into the afterlife. Darker sects further believe that if they remain alive, their love will become mundane and attenuated.

RELATIONS WITH OTHER RELIGIONS

As a former handmaiden of Shelyn, Naderi is still most commonly associated with the Eternal Rose, and the broken relationship between the two goddesses is a popular subject for operas, poems, art, and theological treatises. Naderi avoids her erstwhile patron out of fear and guilt, and Shelyn's attempts to reconcile with her are always thwarted by mysterious circumstances that many theologians believe are the work of another deity. The Lost Maiden still bears considerable affection for Shelyn, and is grieved to be the second loss of a loved one that the goddess of beauty has suffered, after the transformation of Shelyn's brother Dou-Bral into the dark god Zon-Kuthon. The enmity between Naderi and Zon-Kuthon is heightened by the attempts of Naderi's clerics to bring the escape of painless death to victims tortured by Kuthite priests.

Naderi fascinates both Urgathoa and Zyphus. Urgathoa approves of Naderi's insistence that love persists beyond death, emphasizing this agreement between the two in hopes that the Lost Maiden will eventually encourage her followers to pursue the immortality of undeath. Urgathoa's church also holds that suicide can be a noble end, and appreciates the work Naderi's faith does in romanticizing it and removing the stigma around killing oneself. Naderi is wary of the Pallid Princess, for most of her doctrine emphasizes the purity and release of true death over the mundane and shadowy stretches of mortal existence, and she does not see undeath as a superior alternative to life. Yet as Urgathoa offers herself as an elder sister figure who can fill the emptiness left by Naderi's estrangement from Shelyn, the Lost Maiden's resistance is softening.

Zyphus's gospel of nihilism emphasizes the fact that a loved one can be lost to chance at any moment, and he senses that Naderi's obsession with loss accords with his views. He also delights in sowing discord between other divinities, and knows his open courtship of the young goddess worries Shelyn, spurring him to make his overtures all the more extravagant. Naderi, however, finds the resignation inherent in Zyphus's nihilism counter to her views, and continues to spurn him.

REALM

Naderi's realm in the Maelstrom is called the Palace of Love Eternal. It is a place of gardens and groves, filled with clear ponds and streams. Couples who are now forever young stroll along flowery paths, embrace in the shade of wisteria-cloaked arbors, and whisper to one another in ornate gazebos. Despite the beauty and apparent peacefulness, there is a sense of restlessness and dissatisfaction to the place, and most of the couples don't seem content to remain in any of the charming locations for long, roaming from blossom-strewn knoll to sun-dappled clearing and back again as if searching for something they left behind in their mortal lives.

PLANAR ALLIES

Naderi's divine servants are drawn from the souls of those who revered her in life. The following outsiders serve her and answer her faithful's calls via spells such as *planar ally*.

Arden and Lysena (heralds of Naderi): The spirits of the young couple whose deaths triggered Naderi's apotheosis now serve in her realm, and often appear to comfort desperate young lovers who are kept apart. Arden and Lysena appear as comely teenagers dressed in flowing blue robes, and Lysena's left wrist is bound to Arden's right with a red ribbon. They speak in unison and are never seen apart, leading some to theorize their souls somehow melded after death. Indeed, they demonstrate powers similar to those of a single—yet unique and particularly powerful—ember weaver psychopomp; some theologians postulate that they unknowingly achieved their current state thanks to a mysterious plan by Pharasma, even though they actively avoid the Lady of Graves. They leave behind damp footprints and small pools of water as signs that their appearance was not merely a fevered dream.

Phaethor (unique hydrodaemon): Naderi's newest divine servitor is drawn to the growing dark side of her nature. It is known to lurk near bodies of water disguised as a handsome young man, appearing to heartbroken young women who have been spurned by their lovers. Phaethor begins by speaking words of comfort, but is a master at convincing a young woman that her lover's shame and grief over her death will lead him to regret not having appreciated her while she was alive, and that the young woman will be remembered and revered forevermore for her tragic beauty if she simply drowns herself.

Stillheart (unique avoral): An agathion with a long, slim neck, swan's wings, and webbed feat, Stillheart appears to ease the pain of those who have lost a loved one to suicide. Stillheart can appear male, female, or androgynous, but is always a creature of extraordinary beauty and grace. It never speaks—it merely appears to the grieving and sits silently with them—but its presence seems to encourage the bereaved, and most feel a sense of peace and healing after it departs. While Arden and Lysena are better known among mortals, mostly because Stillheart does not speak to identify itself, the avoral is Naderi's closest companion, attempting to assuage her loneliness and keep her despair from growing too great.

Sivanah

Dazzling, inscrutable, alluring, and elusive, Sivanah represents the mystery at the heart of existence. Her church posits there is no such thing as absolute truth, only layers of illusion, and Sivanah herself is a paradox even to her most devout followers, who refer to her as the Endless One. Her holy symbol—a knotted ring of scarves—serves as a metaphor for a cycle of apparitions with neither beginning nor end. Mystics say that when one pulls back Sivanah's seventh and final veil, one finds the first beneath it again. Her priests claim that she has yet to manifest her true form, believing it will be unveiled only during the destruction of reality itself.

THE SEVENTH VEIL
Goddess of illusions, mystery, and reflections

Alignment N

Domains Knowledge, Madness, Magic, Rune, Trickery

Subdomains Deception, Insanity, Memory, Protean, Thought, Wards

Favored Weapon bladed scarf

Centers of Worship Absalom, Irrisen, Nex, Nidal, Numeria, Razmiran

Nationality unknown

Obedience Carry an ordinary scarf or veil and walk through a settlement, making sure you are seen and exchange pleasantries with at least one person. After you reach the settlement's edge, place the scarf or veil over your face so you aren't easily recognizable, and again speak with anyone you encountered before. If your true identity is recognized, you must deny it, providing a false name if necessary. Even if anyone you met sees through your ruse, you gain a +2 sacred or profane bonus on Disguise checks. The type of bonus depends on your alignment—if you're neither good nor evil, you must choose either sacred or profane the first time you perform your obedience, and this choice can't be changed.

> Beneath the first, human guile. Beneath the next, elven wiles. Beneath the third, halfling luck. Beneath the fourth, a gnome's pluck. Beneath the fifth, spiders' craft. Beneath the sixth, naga laughs. Pulled back the last, past my ken. What did I find? The first again.
>
> —Song of Seven Veils

EVANGELIST BOONS

1: Masks and Veils (Sp) *blurred movement*[ACG] 3/day, *invisibility* 2/day, or *major image* 1/day

2: Illusion Expert (Su) Your enemies have a harder time fooling you with illusions. You gain a +4 sacred or profane bonus (of the same type as that provided by your obedience) on Will saves to disbelieve illusions. If you successfully disbelieve an illusion and communicate this fact to others, such viewers gain a +6 bonus (of the same type as above) on their saving throws to disbelieve the illusion.

3: Protection of the Veiled Goddess (Sp) You are skilled at misdirecting your opponents while preparing to do them harm. Once per day as a standard action, you can cast *mislead*. The spell's *greater invisibility* effect lasts a number of rounds equal to your Hit Dice.

EXALTED BOONS

1: Nothing is What It Seems (Sp) *color spray* 3/day, *misdirection* 2/day, or *hide campsite*[APG] 1/day

2: Shared Mask (Sp) As a standard action, you can alter your own appearance and that of up to four willing creatures within a 30-foot radius as per *disguise self*. All the creatures disguised appear to be of a single race or creature type; creatures in the group that could not be disguised as that creature type (such as an animal companion in a group of humanoids) cannot be affected by this ability. This effect lasts 10 minutes per Hit Die you possess.

3: The Protecting Veil (Su) You can shield an area, and those within it, from both mundane and magical observation. As a full-round action, you can meditate to veil an area with an illusion extending in a 30-foot radius around you. During this round, you can't take any other actions, including free or swift actions. The illusion appears as a general concept you envision and can't be changed once in place. The illusion affects only visual observation and scrying; it doesn't create or disguise smells, sounds, or tactile properties. You may maintain the illusion for up to 1 hour, but if you leave the square you were occupying when you initiated it, the illusion is dispelled. The DC to disbelieve the illusion is equal to 10 + your Hit Dice + your Charisma modifier.

SENTINEL BOONS

1: Hard to Pin Down (Sp) *disguise weapon*[ACG] 3/day, *blur* 2/day, or *displacement* 1/day

2: Killer Illusion (Sp) You can channel illusions through your weapon to terrify and even slay your enemies. Once per day, as a free action when you hit with a melee attack, you can cause images of a creature the target most fears to erupt from your weapon right before its eyes. Resolve this effect before rolling damage for the attack; this functions as *phantasmal killer*, and the target can attempt a Will saving throw (DC = 14 + your Charisma modifier) to recognize the image as unreal. On a failed save, the phantasm touches the target, which must then succeed at a Fortitude saving throw (against the same DC) or die from fear. Even if the target succeeds at its Fortitude saving throw, it takes 3d6 points of damage as well as the damage from the successful melee attack. Unlike *phantasmal killer*, this effect cannot be turned upon you if the subject possesses telepathy or is wearing a *helm of telepathy*.

3: Illusive Revenge (Sp) You have learned how to use illusions to torment your enemies even long after battle is over. Once per day, you can cast *phantasmal revenge* (*Pathfinder RPG Advanced Player's Guide* 235) as a spell-like ability upon a recently slain creature, which rises as a ghastly image to seek out its killer. This illusive ghost is always veiled, even if it never was so in life. After the target attempts its Will saving throw (DC = 17 + your Charisma modifier), regardless of whether the attempt was successful, the ghost tears off its veil to reveal an image of the killer's own face.

INTRODUCTION

ACHAEKEK

ALSETA

APSU

BESMARA

BRIGH

DAHAK

GHLAUNDER

GROETUS

GYRONNA

HANSPUR

KURGESS

MILANI

NADERI

SIVANAH

ZYPHUS

SIVANAH AND GNOMES

Gnomes' love of illusion magic and unusual experiences makes Sivanah an attractive deity to many of them. Gnomes refer to her as the Fourth Veil—assumed by others to reference the veil with which Sivanah's gnome form is associated, though gnome clerics claim it is because of some long-forgotten ecclesiastical reasons—and emphasize the playful side of her nature, seeing the interplay between illusion and reality as a game. While most of the goddess's non-gnome worshipers are practitioners of magic, gnome rogues and even fighters may also revere her, using sleight of hand and battle tricks to achieve seemingly magical effects, and wearing knotted scarves (generally in four colors rather than the traditional seven) to honor their patron. Their temples are especially well hidden, often sporting only a scarf in an upstairs window or a rune carved on a gatepost to guide the faithful inside.

For gnomes, Sivanah's concealed form embodies the uncertainty of existence and the exciting lure of hidden truths, while the lifelong pursuit of her eternal mystery offers an escape from tedium, ennui, and the colorless nihilism of the Bleaching. Yet these same qualities also make her a frustrating patron for some gnomes, as her faith doesn't promise answers, but only endless questions. Many gnomes who worship her in their youth find their curiosity stymied in middle age by her inscrutability, and turn to the worship of other deities.

UNDERSTANDING SIVANAH

No living being—mortal or immortal—remembers Sivanah's birth, creation, or ascension to godhood, or can even identify when she first appeared, yet all mortal records of her are relatively recent. None predate Earthfall, suggesting that she was unknown to the Azlanti, though a number of outsiders, when questioned, claim they remember her presence at events before the disaster.

Sivanah is most often recognized by mortals as a goddess of magic—specifically illusion magic. She appears as a veiled figure who takes on a different form as each veil is removed. Under the first shimmering veil appears a human face; yet, when the veil is removed, a gauzy drapery appears to cover an elven woman. Under the third veil is a halfling, and under the fourth, a gnome. For many centuries, the fifth was believed to conceal a cyclops, but in recent centuries, as the power of the cyclopes waned, it has become popular to claim the fifth veil covers an aranea. The sixth veil drapes the form of a naga. No mortal knows what lies behind the seventh.

Visitors to the Maelstrom who have attempted to locate Sivanah's ever-moving realm speculate the goddess is hiding from a number of protean choruses, either because she possesses something that belongs to them or because her true nature provokes their enmity. Others believe she was once a keketar, a risen demon, or a fallen azata. In recent years, because of the high number of fetchling worshipers in Sivanah's church, theologians have begun to claim the Seventh Veil originally hailed from the Shadow Plane. The only truth people can agree on is that she appears to be female, though even that may be an illusion.

THE CHURCH

Most individuals have had occasion or need to conceal the truth at some point in their lives, and even the most honest can feel the allure of daydreams, stories, and other excursions into the illusions of the imagination. Sivanah's faithful elevate this understanding to a worshipful level. Most of Sivanah's rituals take place at dawn and twilight, honoring the way these transitional periods alter familiar places and cloak landscapes in mystery. It is traditional to visit her holy places and offer prayers at these times.

Those who worship the Seventh Veil do so for myriad reasons, but usually with the awareness that they will be met with distrust because of their deity's enigmatic nature. For worshipers who value the mysteries at the heart of existence, or those who must disguise some element of their being for their own safety, the beauty and power of their faith is well worth the price.

Sivanah's church is extremely mysterious to non-practitioners. While other deities also hold sway over secrets, Sivanah's church is notoriously tight-lipped about its true beliefs and most of its practices, and instructs its members to use prevarication and misleading half-truths when they are questioned about its nature. Many clergy cloak themselves in both veils of illusion and literal veils, disguising their voices and hiding their true appearance, which exacerbates the suspicion that the church harbors nefarious goals (as does Sivanah's trickster role in many folktales and myths).

The church has a centralized governing body, called the Seven Masks, but the identities of its seven members are concealed, even from each other, and their instructions and doctrinal decisions are conveyed through such circuitous routes that most members in the chain of command are unknown to the others. The majority of instruction comes from the clergy, but Sivanah herself sometimes speaks directly to her followers through reflections in mirrors and pools of water, or even through their own shadows—though, as her followers point out, there is no way to know for sure that these messages come from the goddess and not from other clergy members.

Despite the unease that such secrecy provokes from those on the outside, the church manages to allay some suspicion and gain goodwill and acceptance through

the holiday of Seven Veils; this colorful, open-armed, and often riotous event celebrates local culture and the traditions and features of each race associated with Sivanah's first six veils. Sivanah's clergy cloak their town or city and its inhabitants in light illusions that conceal little, only enhancing the beauty of the surroundings and the people, and contribute their abilities to comic performances, generous-spirited practical jokes, and other entertainment. The clergy even remove their veils for the festival's duration—though whether they then cloak their true faces in illusion is the subject of much speculation and debate.

TEMPLES AND SHRINES

Sivanah's temples often appear to be something else entirely, for followers of the Seventh Veil pride themselves on hiding things in plain sight. A popular art gallery might contain a temple, as might a stately manor or a simple eatery. Many of these buildings do serve their apparent purposes, but for others, their disguises are only that. Some temples disguise their entrances behind layers of illusion magic. In cities, doors are sometimes placed in alleyways where the position of the walls hides them from passersby, or thick vines are hung before entrances to forest temples to distract the eye.

The interiors of these temples can be intentionally disorienting, for Sivanah's worshipers believe one must learn to distrust one's eyes before being able to discern greater truths of the heart and mind. A temple may be oddly shaped to distort perspective and give the impression that people standing on one side of a room are twice as tall as those on the other, or have trompe l'oeil murals or floor designs that present doorways or drop-offs where none exist. Many have no interior walls, separating rooms with shimmering veils or using movable mirrors to direct light to areas intended for different purposes when they are in use. Most have a room or large area that can double as a theater.

A PRIEST'S ROLE

Priests of Sivanah run the gamut from playful illusionists to inscrutable veiled mystics. Some don't bother hiding their own appearance or nature, focusing on creating chimerical works of beauty or terror. Others conceal their race, gender, and true nature, with each false surface layered above another, revealing nothing real even to those with whom they are closest.

In gnome culture, worship of Sivanah revolves less around concealment of the self and more around the creation of sights and sounds to add color and excitement to areas where life threatens to grow dull. Gnome clerics of Sivanah enjoy presenting themselves as companions of fearsome creatures such as dragons or giants, though their intimidating protectors are often strangely shy, appearing rarely and saying little. Halfling clerics are also known to use these tricks, especially in areas where halflings are enslaved or oppressed. Naga, aranea, and elven clerics tend to focus on the mystical aspects of Sivanah's worship, using illusions to reveal deeper truths, and exploring whether absolute truth even exists.

Humans in Sivanah's clergy typically choose to devote their lives to the goddess for reasons as diverse as their own cultures. Many serve criminal organizations such as thieves' guilds, or try to make life better for populations that are marginalized or distrusted. Some pursue mysticism, while others use their talents to create works of art, or provide their services to theater troupes and carnivals. A few offer their services as spies.

While most clerics of Sivanah hail from one of the six races represented by the goddess's six veils, the Seventh Veil also has a strong following among fetchlings who make their home on the Material Plane. Fetchlings' affinity for the Seventh Veil has given rise to stories that she originated from this race, a wildly controversial idea potentially supported by the absence of any mention of the goddess in surviving texts that predate Earthfall.

Clerics of Sivanah spend part of their time tending to other adherents of their faith, but most also sell their services to anyone who requires disguises or illusions. To the surprise of those who do not worship the Seventh Veil, clerics of Sivanah often have strong feelings about the legitimacy of government, though they may not align with those of other Sivanans. Roughly half see a strong, centralized government as an essential tool of civilization, and may offer their aid to rulers by playing upon national myths, creating rituals and ceremonies to enhance

prestige and control over the populace, and disguising the less glamorous or palatable aspects of what they must do to retain power. A recent scandal in Ustalav was sparked by the discovery that the local church of Sivanah had been working with the ruling family of the country for generations to seed legends supporting their rule. The other faction of Sivanans sees large-scale rulership over others as illegitimate, though they recognize the necessity of local governments and guilds, and use their abilities to help like-minded individuals hide their activities from the prying eyes of the state.

Clerics of Sivanah can prepare *ghost sound* as an orison, *silent image* as a 1st-level spell, *hypnotic pattern* as a 2nd-level spell, and *veil* as a 6th-level spell.

ADVENTURERS

Sivanah's faith attracts both those with a strong streak of curiosity and those with something to hide. Many adventurers who worship her are driven to explore because they feel their homes can no longer offer them the mystery they crave. Even when they meet with great success, such individuals rarely remain settled for long, striking out for new vistas each time their surroundings become overly familiar.

Some of Sivanah's faithful have secrets they wish to conceal. Many have done something that violates the laws or mores of the lands in which they live, while others have a tragedy from which they wish to separate themselves. For many who have turned to the Seventh Veil to hide something that endangers them or causes them pain, discovery can send them fleeing, or the promise of redemption, a cure, or a solution to their problems can cause them to take up the adventuring life.

Adventurers who pray to Sivanah may evoke respect, curiosity, and even admiration from their companions, but most are slow to gain their partners' trust. Many adventurers are predisposed to believe their Sivanan associates might use their abilities to stealthily take more than their fair share of the loot, avoid putting themselves at risk in dangerous battles, and so on.

CLOTHING

Worshipers of the Seventh Veil are fond of scarves made of seven pieces of fabric in different colors knotted in a circle. Gnome spellcasters who revere Sivanah often dye their hair in four or seven different colors.

Among wealthy worshipers, bracelets made of seven different metals have become popular tokens, noticeable only to the most observant and usually recognized only by other Sivanans. Sivanah's priests usually wear veils and layered clothing that hide their shape and features, and may go out of their way to give false impressions of their race, gender, and other identifying characteristics.

HOLY TEXTS

Sivanah's holy texts are almost always hidden in other books, either in ink that appears only in sunlight, or more often as every seventh word in an otherwise unremarkable volume on an unrelated subject. Sivanah's priests teach that each text has four levels of meaning: the literal or surface meaning, the symbolic meaning, the personal meaning an author brings to it, and the personal meaning a reader brings to it. Somewhere in the combination of these four layers lies truth.

Beyond the Seventh Veil: This meditation on the nature of truth is one of the best-known Sivanan holy texts, and it concludes that real truth does not exist. Some scholars even believe it clandestinely reveals Sivanah's true identity, though this idea is blasphemous in some circles.

HOLIDAYS

Sivanan holidays are typically kept secret among her faithful. Only the following holiday is known as a time of celebration to all of Sivanah's church.

Seven Veils: In most parts of the Inner Sea region, this holiday takes place on 7 Neth. It is a day-long celebration of diversity filled with dancing, feasting, and courting. The evening traditionally closes out with the Seven Veil masquerade, a ball wherein the participants wear disguises. At the end of the ball, the participants remove their partners' disguises, often with unpredictable or delightfully awkward results. Sivanan worshipers count this among their most sacred days and conduct secretive rituals, the details of which they conceal just as carefully as any of their activities.

APHORISMS

The sayings of Sivanah's faithful praise cleverness, extol the beauty of illusions, and meditate upon the nature of truth.

Don't Try to Blind a Veiled One: The idea that one shouldn't attempt to con a con artist has given rise to any number of variants of this saying, but worshipers of Sivanah make it their own with the suggestion that a lifetime spent misleading others gives one special insight into seeing through others' attempts at deception.

Veils upon Veils: Sivanah's faith suggests that there may be no such thing as ultimate truth, and that the idea of such is an illusion. This aphorism reminds her worshipers that if they believe they have found absolute truth, they are most assuredly fooled by an illusion.

RELATIONS WITH OTHER RELIGIONS

Despite her popularity with gnomes, Sivanah's relationship with Nivi Rhombodazzle is distant, though mutually respectful. Neither goddess objects to gnomes paying homage to both of them. Sivanah is fascinated by the empyreal lord Arshea's refusal to be categorized into a single gender, and Arshea's followers have studied methods of ambiguous self-presentation with Sivanah's clergy.

As for the more popular Inner Sea gods, Nethys finds her especially intriguing, and the two sometimes cautiously share magical knowledge, with each attempting to maintain the upper hand. Desna doesn't entirely trust her, but admires the beauty of Sivanah's illusions, seeing them as dreamlike, and Sivanah is intrigued by the mysteries surrounding the ancient goddess. Shelyn likewise is drawn to the Seventh Veil's capacity to spin gorgeous figments, and sometimes goes to her for inspiration. Cayden Cailean has long pursued Sivanah, but thus far has had no luck in attracting her interest.

Sivanah also maintains a cordial relationship with Norgorber, and their attempts to manipulate one another often have an air of playfulness about them, as if the two deities were engaged in a game. They plot together as often as they plot against one another, though the fruition of their schemes often goes unnoticed or is unrecognizable. Rumors abound that Sivanah is helping Norgorber conceal a truth about his nature or history.

The Seventh Veil's most adversarial relationship is with Zon-Kuthon. She views the Midnight Lord's use of shadows as a corruption of their true purpose, and sometimes takes control of the shadows his clerics wield, causing them to act in unexpected ways. Zon-Kuthon has made her worship an offense punishable by torture and death within Nidal. Despite the danger, a few of Sivanah's most daring clerics remain within Nidal's borders, for her church views residence in Nidal as the greatest test of a cleric's abilities at disguise. These Nidalese clerics attempt to subtly undermine Zon-Kuthon's hold over the nation and lure other Nidalese away from his worship.

While most deities regard Razmir with contempt or disdainful amusement, the Seventh Veil seems to have an incomprehensible interest in the Living God. Whether this is simply because she admires the boldness and cleverness of his illusory godhood, or because she is playing a deeper game, Sivanah is silent on her reasons for supporting his false church. Veiled witches from Irrisen serve as her most frequent emissaries to Razmiran.

REALM

As mutable and mysterious as the Maelstrom's sea of creative and destructive potential upon which it floats, Sivanah's realm never appears in the same place twice. Both visitors to the plane and its native proteans may pass through it without recognizing it; save for a preponderance of mirrors, the plane changes its appearance as often as it changes location. Her divine servitors and the souls of her worshipers appear to be able to find it without trouble, but whether the Seventh Veil gives them special guidance is unknown to her living followers.

PLANAR ALLIES

Sivanah's divine servitors are unique and of unidentifiable origins. The following beings respond to *planar ally* and similar spells cast by Sivanah's faithful.

Ai (herald of Sivanah): Like its mistress, this unique trumpet archon often appears as a veiled figure, but the shimmering fabric that swathes it moves in ways that obfuscate the individual beneath the veils. Ai never speaks, instructing the faithful through gestures or wordless empathy. It sometimes appears to observe high-level clergy performing great works of illusion, and it has been known to contribute a bit of its own enhancement when it seems especially impressed. It also occasionally manifests in response to what would otherwise be unsuccessful summoning spells by worshipers of Zon-Kuthon, showing up in a form they would expect and obeying their commands until a critical moment, when it disappears or aids their foes. How or why Ai has left its native plane of Heaven to serve Sivanah in the Maelstrom and beyond is yet another of the faith's many mysteries.

The Flickering Man (unique Huge lightning elemental): A strange lightning elemental (*Pathfinder RPG Bestiary 2* 116), the Flickering Man oddly takes the shape of a tall, thin humanoid man when he appears. He speaks in a highly formal, often flowery manner that can distract the unwary from the fact that his statements rarely contain any useful information. He prefers offerings of six identical valuable objects, which he absorbs before speaking.

The Severed Mask (unique shae): Cloaked in shadow, the Severed Mask wears a white mask with a crack down the center from which darkness leaks. This shae (*Pathfinder RPG Bestiary 3* 242) speaks in an echoing, sibilant whisper, and answers direct questions only with other questions. These responses often encourage the questioner to look at problems from a revelatory new angle. She gladly accepts gifts of broken or damaged artwork.

INTRODUCTION

ACHAEKEK

ALSETA

APSU

BESMARA

BRIGH

DAHAK

GHLAUNDER

GROETUS

GYRONNA

HANSPUR

KURGESS

MILANI

NADERI

SIVANAH

ZYPHUS

Zyphus

Zyphus is said to have been the first mortal to die an accidental and meaningless death. When his soul appeared in Pharasma's Boneyard, he cursed the goddess and refused to accept her judgment. His wrath and the unique circumstances of his death bent destiny and granted him divinity. Now, Zyphus is the god of accidental deaths, especially tragic and pointless ones. Cruel, vindictive, petty, and nihilistic, Zyphus has few worshipers, but is feared in most lands as the always-looming specter of unexpected demise. A malevolent, hateful force, he is responsible for many unexplained, senseless deaths—he seeks to bring ruin and sadness into the world and rob mortals of hope and their faith in fate, fortune, and divine succor.

THE GRIM HARVESTMAN

God of accidental death, graveyards, and tragedy

Alignment NE

Domains Death, Destruction, Evil, Plant, War

Subdomains Blood, Catastrophe, Daemon, Decay, Murder, Undead

Favored Weapon heavy pick

Centers of Worship Galt, Nidal, Numeria, Qadira, the Sodden Lands, Taldor, Ustalav, Varisia

Nationality Keleshite

Obedience Spend an hour sitting on the grave of someone who suffered an accidental death. You must reflect on how chance has wronged you and vocally reject the influence of any gods associated with these wrongs. If no suitable grave exists, spend an hour telling strangers how their religious beliefs and hopes for a just afterlife are folly and of no consequence. Alternatively, you can write this screed and post it in a public place within a settlement. If you're away from civilization, you can instead spend an hour sabotaging a path, bridge, tool, or other device so that it's dangerous for the next person who uses it. You gain a +4 profane bonus on Craft (traps) or Disable Device checks, chosen when you complete the obedience.

Everyone you love and everything you care for may be taken from you at a moment's notice. The young, the beautiful, and the rich—all are prey to the indifferent, clutching hand of chance.

—*Letters of Harsh Truth*

EVANGELIST BOONS

1: Champion of Cruel Chance (Sp) *deathwatch* 3/day, *false life* 2/day, or *healing thief*[UC] 1/day

2: Resiliency (Ex) Once per day, you can gain a number of temporary hit points equal to your Hit Dice, lasting for 1 minute. Activating this ability is an immediate action that can be performed only when you would be brought below 0 hit points, and can be used to prevent you from dying. If you have the resiliency ability from another source, you can activate these abilities separately or as part of the same immediate action.

3: Tragic Minion (Su) By spending 1 minute praying over the corpse of a humanoid opponent or a humanoid who has died a tragic death, you can summon an allip (*Pathfinder RPG Bestiary 3* 12) to serve you. Unlike a normal allip, this allip is of an alignment that matches yours, and has a number of hit points equal to half your total. It receives a +4 bonus on Will saves to halve the damage from channeled positive energy, and it can't be turned or commanded. This allip serves as a companion to you and can communicate intelligibly with you despite its madness. You can dismiss it as a standard action. If the allip is destroyed or dismissed, you can't summon another for 7 days. This ability allows you to have only one allip companion at a time.

EXALTED BOONS

1: Catalyst of Destruction (Sp) *break*[APG] 3/day, *find traps* 2/day, or *spiked pit*[APG] 1/day

2: Ever Vigilant (Su) Protected by Zyphus from a surprising death while you still have work to do for him, you're resistant to effects that attack your life force or would affect you before you have a chance to react. You are protected by *death ward*, except the immunity to energy drain ends after it has prevented a number of negative levels equal to your exalted level; this resets when you next perform your obedience. You gain a +2 profane bonus on saving throws against effects that occur before your first turn in combat.

3: Visitors from Abaddon (Sp) Once per day as a standard action, you can summon a pair of greater ceustodaemons (*Pathfinder RPG Bestiary 2* 65) as if with *summon monster II*, and gain telepathy with them to a range of 100 feet. The ceustodaemons follow your commands perfectly for 1 round per Hit Die you possess before vanishing back to their home on Abaddon. The ceustodaemons don't follow commands that would cause them to perform overly good acts or save mortal lives other than your own, and they immediately vanish if your orders contradict these restrictions.

SENTINEL BOONS

1: Walking Disaster (Sp) *bungle*[UM] 3/day, *spontaneous immolation*[UC] 2/day, or *deadly juggernaut*[UC] 1/day

2: Tragic Accident (Su) You have a deep understanding of the Grim Harvestman's lordship over accidental death, and can unleash these accidents on your enemies. Once per day as part of a successful attack, you can target your opponent with either *inflict critical wounds* or *poison* as a free action. The DC for this ability is equal to 10 + 1/2 your Hit Dice + your Charisma modifier. You don't have to declare the use of this ability until you know the attack is successful.

3: Unfairness of the World (Su) Once per day, you can channel all of your outrage through your weapon, afflicting your opponent with deadly negative energy. You must declare your use of this ability before you roll an attack. On a hit, the target gains a number of negative levels equal to 3 + 1/2 your Hit Dice unless it succeeds at a Fortitude saving throw (the DC for this ability is the same as your tragic accident DC). If you openly wear an unholy symbol of Zyphus, the saving throw DC to resist this effect increases by 2.

ZYPHUS'S ANTIPALADIN CODE

The antipaladins of Zyphus are stealthy, and in emulation of their cruel patron deity, they're obsessed with sowing death at the most unexpected and shocking moments. Few appear openly on the field of battle except when they impersonate followers of Gorum to incite maximum collateral damage in a skirmish or war. Although all adhere to Zyphus's tenets, they vary in which parts of the code they emphasize. These tenets include the following adages.

- Happiness is ignorance. I will never hide the truth of anguish.
- I am an agent of unpredictable death. I will announce my murderous intentions only to Zyphens and those I will immediately kill.
- Mercy is pointless. I will not stay my hand when I can slay my enemies.
- Prophecies are empty promises. I will pay no heed to fortune-telling.
- Tragedy must spread. I will first hurt those whose pain will also hurt many others, whether because they are beloved or because they will wreak reckless vengeance.

UNDERSTANDING ZYPHUS

Unlike Pharasma, who has careful, fated plans for each mortal soul, Zyphus represents chance and the unexpected aspects of mortality. It's said that every accidental death adds to his strength, and that he may someday grow powerful enough to usurp Pharasma's place. Others preach that every soul he claims allows him a brief respite from his rage as he savors its former mortality, and that these shallow sips of life motivate him to keep reaching for more.

Also known as the Grim Harvestman, Zyphus both loves and hates his worshipers, known as Zyphens. On the one hand, they constantly remind him of his divine nature, feeding his ego and furthering his goals in the mortal world. But the petty deity envies his followers' mortal lives, and resents them for having what he no longer has. Communication with his followers is brief, terse, and often full of bile, encouraging ruthless actions; any apparent kindness in him is merely a lull as he seethes with quiet anger before the next outburst. Some among his faithful believe that once he usurps Pharasma's place, he will allow all souls to wander the planes unsorted and reincarnate himself as a mortal with no memories of his prior existence.

Zyphus appears as a gloomy figure clad in hooded black robes decorated with bones. His face is a gaunt, pale nightmare with a distended, screaming mouth and hollow eye sockets grown over by translucent membranes of skin. He wields a heavy pick reputed to be made from his mortal body's bones. Zyphus's feet are hidden beneath his robes, and he never leaves tracks when he passes.

Zyphus shows his pleasure with the sound of skeletal laughter, the cracking of knuckles, the sensation of a cold but comforting hand on the shoulder, or momentary images of a vulture's wing. When he wishes to convey his anger, ropes fray, hard materials creak and snap, hands become sweaty and slippery, and vultures gather.

THE CHURCH

Zyphus's priests are primarily clerics or inquisitors, though a few oracles of bones blame him for their curses. His faith is widespread but small. His cultists tend to be more populous in Numeria, where old technology often malfunctions; in Galt, where one is always just a slip of the tongue away from a beheading; and in Nidal, where brooding evil and fatalism are the norm. Lesser cults exist in Qadira, the Sodden Lands, Taldor, Ustalav, and Varisia.

Most of Zyphus's worshipers have suffered some great tragedy or loss, such as a loved one's death or the loss of a limb in an accident. Rather than the victims learning from the experience, healing, and moving on, their pain has grown into anger, bitterness, and cynicism, and they seek to punish others just as they feel they were wronged. Embracing the idea that the universe is ruled by chance rather than some grand plan, Zyphens work to convince others to reject their misplaced faith in other gods. Many learn how to build traps and orchestrate convoluted "accidents" to kill others in Zyphus's name, believing such deaths consign their victims' souls to him. However, most lack the courage to actually harm others, and are content to engage in tirades belittling the achievements, successes, loves, and victories of others as pointless and temporary. Some shout these admonishments at passersby in the street, while others take a more cowardly path and write out their grievances, delivering them to the recipient anonymously or posting them in public for all to read.

Worship services mix percussion (usually with rattles or a xylophone with bars of shaped bone), hissing chants, libations of blood, and the rolling of knucklebone dice. If the ceremony takes place near a dungeon or another dangerous location, cultists might release a prisoner into it on holidays, making bets on how long the wretch will survive before being killed by a trap or creature.

The cult of the Grim Harvestman is organized in independent cells, each of which treats a city or region as its sovereign territory. A cell is led by a powerful leader with a reputation for many kills—all cultists, even those from other cells, respect these leaders. Priests of high enough rank are called Harvestmasters. Unlike solitary members of this religion, those who join a cell usually remove themselves from civilization and devote their full attention to orchestrating small accidents and disasters to feed their master's will. A few cells overtly assault the established order, planning and executing large-scale disasters such as ferry sinkings, fires that obliterate whole neighborhoods, and building collapses. Such cults usually have the resources to procure powerful magic to aid their work, creating traps with spells such as *fabricate, move earth, create pit, stone shape,* and so on.

Zyphus doesn't care about mortal marriage or families—his followers may take spouses and have children, but are keenly aware that they might lose these people at any time. As a result, most in the church are either extremely committed to their loved ones (and are more devastated at their deaths) or coolly remote with their emotions (the better to survive the inevitable grief).

TEMPLES AND SHRINES

Zyphus's church doesn't build permanent temples, preferring to make use of existing spaces. Often, his worshipers hold court in graveyards or mausoleums that have fallen from other gods' favor or are otherwise no longer hallowed ground. Many graveyards are built with carvings on gate arches, vault roofs, and even gravestones to ward away Zyphus's attention, and the god's followers go out of their way to deface such marks to instead welcome him. If the cultists intend to use that facility in the future, they may renovate it or re-consecrate any dead buried there in Zyphus's name. Zyphens place deadly traps around their sites of worship to harm the unwary, often in ways that mock the sites' former dedicatees.

Shrines to the Grim Harvestman are typically stolen and defaced headstones or bouquets of bones left at the sites of meaningless deaths. If such a death occurs at a building that is later torn down or demolished, cultists bury these tokens in the earth, or—if the site is being rebuilt—within the foundation of the new structure so the land remains cursed with the lingering memory of that death.

A PRIEST'S ROLE

A priest of the Grim Harvestman is expected to evangelize, converting others to the cause through harsh words or harsher lessons. Because those lessons usually involve deliberate "accidents" that cause injury or death, Zyphen priests must pursue their activities in secret to avoid retaliation or arrest. When speaking with folk who have suffered loss, a Zyphen priest acts as a guide or counselor, explaining that life is random, capricious, and unfair, and that accepting this fact makes existence more bearable.

City-bound priests often take menial jobs where they can subtly sabotage buildings, such as painting a building with a mixture of varnish and lamp oil, weakening support struts in theater balconies, or using wet sand instead of mortar for stone walls. Rural priests place steel shanks in grain mills to create sparks, replace hunters' bug-repelling oils with ones that attract predators, or pour impurities into molten ingots or contaminants into wells. There are few druids of Zyphus, but his priests with the Plant domain usually work with or around plants in some capacity, especially those feeding on death.

Some Zyphen priests are skilled at crafting functional-looking but secretly defective items for high-risk professions, notably weapons and armor for city guards and adventurers. Such items appear normal, but actually have the fragile quality (*Pathfinder RPG Ultimate Combat* 146). If the item fails, the bearer is likely to die and be unable to return to the priest with a complaint about inferior merchandise. Other priests work undercover in hospitals, quietly dispatching sick or injured patients—making

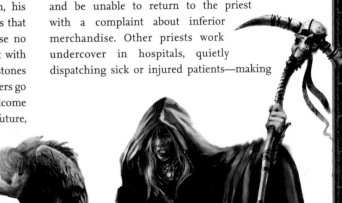

it seem like they've taken a sudden turn for the worse—or administering dangerous experimental "medicines" that actually sicken or kill patients.

Because their agenda is so dark and hostile, few priests reveal their faith. They typically hold mundane professions, and either keep their divine spellcasting hidden or pretend to be of a different faith altogether. Brigh and Torag are common choices for this purpose because of those religions' shared focus on crafting; Pharasma is another favorite because of the overlapping interest in death and the opportunity to perform blasphemies in the name of the Lady of Graves.

Zyphus's clerics are usually trained in Craft (alchemy, carpentry, stonemasonry, or traps), Knowledge

(engineering), or Profession (architect, engineer, or miner). Depending on their other interests and work, they may have ranks in Bluff, Heal, or Sleight of Hand.

Though Zyphus and his followers are indifferent about the creation of undead (for example, it's uncommon for a Zyphen cleric to act strictly as a necromancer), his priests have a tendency to rise as bodiless undead after their deaths (usually as allips, specters, or wraiths) to continue their work in the mortal world.

Most priests wake, pray, eat, then get to work. Most also pray before sleeping, hoping to ward off a sudden death in the night. Some are frantic in their activities, worried that they'll die before accomplishing their goals. Others are slow-paced and lazy, knowing that death will probably take them when they least expect it, regardless of their actions. Clerics of Zyphus can prepare *daze* and *mage hand* as orisons, *bungle*[UM] as a 1st-level spell, and *spectral hand* as a 2nd-level spell.

ADVENTURERS

Adventuring is a risky profession; as a result, some Zyphens find themselves attracted to adventuring like flies to rot. Devout Zyphen adventurers usually defer to the leadership of others, preferring to remain in the background and seem helpful when others are watching.

When Zyphens believe they will not be noticed, they seek out ways to spread confusion and death by doing things like rearming disarmed traps, laying their own traps in illogical places, and using unnecessarily destructive spells and items against foes in hopes of causing collateral damage. Many masquerade as devout followers of other gods, much as priests pretend to follow Brigh or Pharasma.

Less-devout Zyphen adventurers can take a manic approach to adventuring, because while all ways of life are innately random and risky, adventuring can provide a quicker path to wealth and power.

CLOTHING

Formal dress for Zyphus's clergy is a helmet or mask in the shape of a skull or a face with pale, distorted features. Skulls and bones are common decorations. Everyday dress for priests and the devout incorporates heavy cloaks that feature the Grim Harvestman's sacred colors of ivory and red. Vulture pets and motifs are also common.

HOLY TEXT

Zyphus has no official text, but he approves of his followers using the following tome to guide their actions.

Letters of Harsh Truth: This book is a collection of revelations about the folly of the gods, the dominance of chance, and how mortals should accept their inevitable and random deaths. It includes responses to specific mortal sufferings—death of a loved one or a beloved pet, loss of a limb, blindness, and so on. A Zyphen priest created the original using automatic writing, and priests often quote it verbatim in the vicious letters they send to strangers.

HOLIDAYS

The major holidays of this informal church were created to mock holidays of the Lady of Graves.

Day of Gritted Teeth: On the fifth day of Pharast, followers of Zyphus go out of their way to inconvenience or harm the devout of Pharasma, committing petty acts such as muddying roads in front of religious processions.

Sinking of Lost Souls: Especially brave cultists single out and attempt to drown a noteworthy priest of Pharasma during her church's Procession of Unforgotten Souls. Several cult cells usually coordinate their efforts on such tasks, for they fear retaliation and desire to spread the blame as much as possible.

APHORISMS

Zyphus's worshipers are fatalistic and practical, and their common phrases are direct and to the point.

Not Today—I Have Work to Do: This is a brief prayer spoken in the morning, asking Zyphus to not claim the supplicant that day, for she serves his cause and it would delay his goals if she died too early.

Let the Grim One Judge You: This is a threat that the listener will suffer a fatal accident (orchestrated either by a mortal or via the direct intervention of the god) and her soul will be sent to Zyphus rather than its intended destination. It is used as a rebuttal to someone winning an argument or prize from the speaker, implying that the victory doesn't matter because death will come soon.

RELATIONS WITH OTHER RELIGIONS

Zyphus is a minor player in the games of the gods—most see him as more of an annoyance or inconvenience than a true threat. His constant predations on souls intended for other divinities is like a single mosquito in a large formal ball—unpleasant and noisy, but difficult to eradicate without detracting from the overall pleasant atmosphere. His most important relationships are with three gods, each for a different reason. Pharasma is his chief adversary. Zyphus is the enemy she doesn't wish to acknowledge; she either can't oppose him directly or is playing at some millennia-long strategy to eliminate him. Urgathoa is his mentor and comrade, with overlapping interests and proximate realms. Zyphus is also trying to form an alliance with Naderi, hoping to turn her toward evil so she accepts his nihilistic view that chance can steal away a loved one at

any time. Because Zyphus's realm is in Abaddon, daemonic cults occasionally have peaceful contact and cooperation with the Harvestman's mortal followers, though his clergy are still wary of the fiend-worshipers.

Zyphus believes that the universe is ruled by chance, not some grand plan; because no gods truly have the answers, mortal faith in them is misplaced. While Zyphus is an agent of random chance, he doesn't seek to promote chaos over order or seek even temporary alliances with forces of liberation, instead working to instill resigned fear and acceptance that a pointless death could come at any time. Abadar, Torag, and Brigh particularly oppose Zyphus because his followers often impersonate their priests while undermining their goals of advancing civilization.

REALM

Zyphus keeps his divine realm within Urgathoa's territory in Abaddon, a massive field of open tombs crafted in mockery of Pharasma's Graveyard of Souls. Long ago, Zyphus had a domain on the Material Plane, but at some point—unprompted and unexpectedly—the daemons of Abaddon set aside a place and offered to let him stay. He willingly (if warily) accepted, and since then no soul destined for his realm has ever been devoured by the native daemons, and his clergy are allowed to travel the River Styx unmolested. The Pallid Princess makes no claim on him, though she appreciates that Zyphen priests often rise as undead to continue their work.

PLANAR ALLIES

Zyphens sometimes call upon daemons to help bring about murderous "accidents." The following allies can be summoned with spells such as *planar ally*.

Enkaytho (fiendish human inquisitor): This olive-skinned priestess has a brilliant mind and enjoys debate and insults. She can turn into gray smoke (as per *gaseous form*) at will, and pretends to be a vampire to unsettle and fool her opponents. She's a 4th-level inquisitor and prefers payment in items that can be used to pacify, heal, or train animals.

Gravedragger (herald of Zyphus): This unique outsider is a cruel prankster who enjoys murdering innocents in unexpected, horrid, ironic, and tragic ways. Gravedragger appears as a vaguely humanoid mass of grave dirt and bones, and wields a heavy pick made of a rib bone punched through a giant's skull. He also takes the form of an old, thin human man with shifty eyes and a sickening, toothy smile. In this form he is known as "Grinning Jack," often shortened to "Grinjack." Gravedragger speaks in a high, mad voice, and is prone to outbursts of cackling. He spends most of his time on Abaddon, exchanging grisly stories with Zyphus's other divine servitors. When left unsupervised, Gravedragger visits Golarion to enact petty revenge, blasphemous murders, and "accidental" deaths.

PATHFINDER
CAMPAIGN SETTING

INNER SEA GODS

UNLOCK THE POWER OF THE GODS!

Put your faith in dozens of awe-inspiring deities and unlock the power of the gods with *Pathfinder Campaign Setting: Inner Sea Gods*, a new 320-page hardcover sourcebook from Paizo.

- Details of the chief gods and goddesses of Golarion; hundreds of demigods; and the histories, dogmas, rituals, and secrets of faith, both religious and profane.

- New prestige classes, subdomains, and spells empower characters to be champions of their deities.

- Legions of otherwordly enemies and allies, from mighty divine servants to the deities' unstoppable heralds.

PATHFINDER
ROLEPLAYING GAME

Be the Life of the Party

ULTIMATE INTRIGUE

Behind the scenes of heroic battles and magical realms lies a seething underbelly of danger and deception. In the pages of *Ultimate Intrigue*, heroes duel with words instead of steel, plot daring heists, and pit their wills against relentless nemeses. This hardcover rules reference for the Pathfinder RPG includes tons of intriguing new subsystems, spells, feats, and magic items perfect for skullduggery and high society. The new vigilante class puts players under the mask, with a secret identity mechanic that allows players to take on two distinct personas!

AVAILABLE NOW!

paizo.com